SELL MORE
&
WORK LESS

Web Selling Techniques Everyone Should Use

- 101 Web Based Sales Tips
- 20 Power Tips to Improve Your Web Selling Skills
- 10 Real-World Examples of Web Based Selling Scenarios
- 8 In-Depth Reviews of Advanced Web Selling Techniques
- 4 Sales Traps To Avoid
- 4-Phase Virtual Sales Process
- How to Build a Prospect Scorecard
- The Virtual Sales Process Workbook

By
ALAN BLUME

With Mike Lauducci, John Scranton and Andrew Blume

WWW.SELLMOREANDWORKLESS.COM
WWW.PROSPECTSCORECARD.COM • WWW.STARTUPSELLING.COM
WWW.STARTMARKETINGTECH.COM • WWW.ALANBLUME.COM

Acknowledgements

Sell More & Work Less is my second book, following *Your Virtual Success*, a traditionally published work (write a couple of chapters and a Query letter, find an agent, create a proposal, find a publisher, sign with the publisher and move into the publishing queue). My first book took over three years to move from the first draft to the bookshelves. *Sell More & Work Less* was a dramatically faster process, and took less than a year to write and publish, though I opted for the new self publishing route as a faster and more efficient go to market strategy. *Sell More & Work Less* was fun and exciting to write, and I was fortunate to have three individuals assisting me, Mike Lauducci, John Scranton and Andrew Blume. Whenever the term, "we" is used in this book, it typically refers to a collaborative effort with my coauthors.

Special thanks are owed to Lisa Coleman who edited the final and complete draft of this book, offering many suggestions and comments. Bruce T. Martin (http://www.brucetmartin.com) did all he could do to create an acceptable author photograph on the back cover. Joe Lauducci provided helpful "in the trenches" sales suggestions as he has now moved to a predominately virtual sales position and is leveraging our web based sales model whenever possible. Peggy Blume, who has her own virtual small business, offered valued insights and suggestions. And thanks to my daughter Amy who provided many relevant suggestions, in her new role as a web marketer and website developer for an environmental organization. Wendy Keller, who provides agent services for authors and speakers, (http://kellermedia. com) and her editor Alex Schnitzler, offered early advice, editing and suggestions. Roy Klein and Andrew Siedlikowski deserve special mention for their design and development efforts with our Prospect Scorecard mobile app. And thanks to the many contractors and clients who help make us successful each and every day.

Contents

Introduction

The Virtual Paradigm Shift And The New Sales Game

Salespeople, small businesses, entrepreneurs, independent professionals, sole proprietors, in fact everyone wants to sell more and do so more efficiently. These days, that means adopting a web leveraged selling model using new Internet tools and techniques to cost effectively compete. Anywhere people can find an Internet connection, they can work and sell, and can do so efficiently – if they understand the new rules, methods and techniques necessary for web based selling. This web paradigm shift is happening now and is accelerating due to several compelling, interconnected forces. These include:

- Increasing Internet accessibility.

- Powerful and inexpensive cloud computing solutions.

- A rapidly expanding population that is embracing the Internet for many uses.

- Significant overhead savings for employers.

- Extremely inexpensive, or even free, real-time communication (e.g., Skype, instant messaging, web meeting and webinar solutions, etc.).

- Social networking tools like LinkedIn, Facebook, Twitter and YouTube.

- Search Engine Optimization (SEO), Search Engine Marketing (SEM).

- Time and money lost related to commuting or on-site visits.

- Continued challenges impacting travel.

These factors are resulting in sweeping changes in many areas of sales and marketing. Traditional selling revolving around planes, trains, automobiles and in person meetings are, or should be, transitioning to a web based qualification and presentation model. This shift is happening now. Take a quick look around your neighborhood and you might find 25 percent of your neighbors already working from home and many of them may be working in a sales or sales related capacity. These virtual salespeople, entrepreneurs, small business owners, contractors, consultants and independent professionals are beginning to take advantage of a better, more efficient, and more profitable model *and* a more flexible lifestyle.

Success means selling more. Whether it's a product, service, or highly intricate solution, everyone seeks improved sales efficiency. Both traditional and virtual businesses know sales equate to success. Yet, the real game changer is web based sales and marketing. Why? Virtual sales and marketing offer an opportunity for businesses to sell their solutions and services better, faster and more efficiently. Yet, very little information is widely available about virtual sales, embracing the sales process remotely using the many tools available on the Internet.

Sell More & Work Less: Web Selling Techniques Everyone Should Use will help sales and business professionals quickly learn and apply many new virtual sales tips and techniques to improve their sales efficacy, allowing for more free time and a better lifestyle. Simply said, allowing salespeople to sell more and work less. My 4-Phase Virtual Sales Process facilitates the transition to a web based sales process, with greater profit potential, improved methods of selling and a more flexible business and personal lifestyle. You can replicate the 4-Phase Virtual Sales Process to create your own tailored sales process using the techniques explained in this web selling tips book. My web based sales model levels the playing field. It allows almost anyone or any business to more effectively sell against better-funded or better-known organizations. We all know that the fastest *and* cheapest distribution solution wins. The horse drawn wagon was replaced by the locomotive, clipper ships by steamboats, the telegraph by the telephone, and the book will soon be replaced by the eReader. If there is a better, faster and cheaper distribution solution, businesses will embrace the change or face extinction. Think of Borders versus Amazon or Blockbuster versus Netflix. Find a better, faster and cheaper way to do something and you'll likely find a winning solution.

This book explains how to leverage new Internet tools and techniques to cost effectively compete without investing in infrastructure. For example, leveraging cloud computing tools allows small businesses or entrepreneurs to procure sophisticated, yet easy-to-use computer solutions for pennies a day. Cloud computing refers to online tools like Web meeting solutions or e-marketing solutions, which allow anyone to sell globally without needing to install servers, expensive computer networks or invest in computer-savvy staff. If you're not yet familiar with this type of jargon, refer to Appendix 1 to review commonly used sales and Internet terms.

Our sales tips are gleaned from a proven process, including how to deliver effective virtual presentations and solution demonstrations, virtual elevator pitches, effective Web seminars and online meetings. You will learn how to respond faster and deliver better service at lower costs and on a more flexible schedule than if travel were involved. Truly polished and professional virtual presentations help ensure your prospects will be more effectively converted into customers. You will learn how to create effective virtual prospect lists to fill the virtual pipeline and to master the elements of virtual collaboration. Combining these tips into a coherent four-phase sales process helps you create your own custom sales methodology for business-to-business (B2B) or business-to-consumer (B2C) sales, simple or complex sales, and local, national or even international markets. In the last chapter, you will find a guide to help you create your own customized virtual sales process for use in any virtual or partially virtual business.

Real-World Results

This simple-to-learn model has resulted in large six figure sales to people whom I never met face to face, and many small deals that never would be profitable in a traditional business. My virtual team frequently closes a wide variety of business deals including many marketing and lead generation projects, which range in value from under $10,000 to over $100,000, and do so without ever leaving their homes, be they in Massachusetts, New York or Nevada.

Small businesses, entrepreneurs, small office/home office professionals, and even burned out salespeople seeking a better business opportunity and lifestyle can use these sales tips to drive sales virtually and more profitably. Millions of people's lives can be transformed by learning to sell more effectively and efficiently. Even if they don't call themselves "salespeople," everyone is trying to sell something to someone. Today, they all need current, web selling skills to succeed.

Rethinking Brick-and-Mortar

There are well over 100 million small businesses across the globe. These businesses need to embrace the virtual sales process to be successful and shed their traditional, physical, brick-and-mortar model. Of course these web based techniques are not limited to small businesses, larger businesses can also reap the benefits, but will they be agile enough and sufficiently progressive to take advantage of these techniques? Sales meetings and presentations should be virtual whenever possible, salespeople and business owners should reach for their mouse, not a car key, when they seek to speak with a prospective client. This transition takes planning and practice, but can be accomplished by anyone. This book is written for anyone trying to sell anything better, faster and more efficiently. If you're not effectively leveraging web based selling, you're going to fall behind, and will do so very quickly.

In the world of business, a web based sales evolution is happening. Those who adapt will win the day. This book delivers the sales tips you need to evolve your old school brick-and-mortar operation into a state-of-the-art web based selling machine.

Virtual Sales Primer

Sell More & Work Less includes 101 valuable Internet sales techniques, tips and examples. Each chapter has 20 to 30 important tips organized into a logical and repeatable 4-Phase Virtual Sales Process. You can replicate these results by creating your own tailored sales process in Chapter 5. There are 20 Power Tips, 10 Real-World Scenarios, 8 In-Depth Reviews, and 4 Watch-Out Tips which can be reviewed chronologically, following the 4-Phase Virtual Sales Process, or you can jump to an area of specific need, Virtual Presentations for example. Ultimately you want to ensure you are taking advantage of all the web based selling techniques available to you, from qualifying a prospect to creating a Prospect Scorecard, to optimizing your web presentations for maximum impact.

All special tips included in this book are accented with an icon for easy reference:

 Power Tips indicate valuable sales techniques to benefit the reader.

 In-Depth Reviews include best practices on topics such as successful on-line presentations, how to create a virtual Path to Purchase (P2P), and how to create and use a backward timeline.

 Real-World Scenarios detail valuable insights and link specific tips to real-world examples. You will learn about contact management solutions; virtual go-to market strategies; and, how to understand visual and verbal clues to help you close more sales.

 Watch-Out Tips will help you avoid hidden yet important obstacles.

The 4-Phase Virtual Sales Process can be used by essentially any business, sales professional, entrepreneur or home-office-based business. This process offers a proven formula to improve selling. The four phases (identify, qualify, present and close) create a fundamental virtual selling foundation, which this book gradually builds upon. *Sell More & Work Less* is written in an easy-to-read and user friendly format to help you rapidly learn and understand this web based process. *Sell More & Work Less* can be used to advance your current sales efforts into a more profitable and more virtual process.

Definition of Terms

Virtual selling means different things to different people. From my perspective, "virtual selling" means identifying, qualifying, presenting and closing sales without physically meeting the prospective buyer. I created a 4-Phase Virtual Sales Process to better define this Internet leveraged selling methodology. Does your business need to be completely virtual? The simple answer is no. Try selecting aspects of your business that lend themselves to Internet-based selling and leverage the improved margins and efficiencies to be found with those business elements. For example, perhaps you sell consulting services and need to review your offerings with prospective clients as an early step in your qualification process. Does this have to be done in person? Can you substitute a web meeting or Skype call for an on-site meeting? If you're an insurance agent or financial planner can you qualify the prospect and review documents in a web meeting before investing in an on-site meeting? Remember, the more virtual your business, the more profitable and efficient.

As we discuss the nuances of the 4-Phase Virtual Sales Process, you'll encounter many business and sales terms, some of which might be foreign to you. If you're in need of a detailed definition, take a glance at Appendix 1 in the back of this book where we have defined over 50 of these Web-based sales, marketing and Internet business terms.

Using the Tips

As you review our virtual sales tips, you will find a chronological order applicable to many types of sales cycles. Of course, every sales cycle has unique attributes and challenges. Depending on your type of product, service or solution, the steps in your process might be succinct or extensive. The goal with the 4-Phase Virtual Sales Process is for you to think about the process. You do not want, or need, an onerous process. However, you should be aware that there is a process and ensure you're addressing the key elements in your unique sales cycle. Splitting your process into four phases (identify, qualify, present and close) allows you to understand and address the requirements of each phase, ensuring a better likelihood of success as you compete for each opportunity.

We suggest that you review these tips in sequence, browsing the tips you understand well, and focusing on those which you have not yet addressed or considered. At the end of each chapter, note the tips which you feel will be most helpful, or provide the greatest opportunity for your business. These will help you in Chapter 5, when you build your own 4-Phase Virtual Sales Process.

Now, let's begin at a logical beginning. Let's ensure you are fishing in the right pond and identifying targeted suspects which will yield in-profile prospects for your business. Filtering suspects effectively at the top of your sales funnel will result in greater efficiencies as you progress in your sales process.

Chapter 1

Phase 1: Identify

There is a virtual sales storm brewing and its epic proportions will change the sales landscape for years to come. It will change the way the world sells their products, services and solutions. And for all entrepreneurs, small office/home office (SOHOs) professionals, emerging businesses, sales professionals and existing small businesses who prepare themselves for this storm, the result could be a David and Goliath ending with entrepreneurs, small businesses and Internet-savvy sales professionals winning the day. Web based selling is more flexible, profitable, efficient and cost effective. Virtual allows small business and home-office-based businesses and salespeople to take advantage of powerful Internet business and sales tools for a truly nominal investment. These tools and methods allow salespeople and small businesses to efficiently outsell the giants, while maintaining a low overhead operation.

Once you have determined the product, service or solution you wish to sell (we'll typically refer to these as your "solution" for the remainder of this book), all sales efforts should begin by identifying your target profile, building your prospect list, and carrying your message to people who can and will buy. It's best to refer to your initial target prospect list as a "suspect list" because prospects should really be construed as qualified suspects. Whether you're a new startup, an emerging business or an established business, it is still worthwhile to review your suspect list. Starting from the basics will help you develop a high-quality prospect pipeline. Let's review a few of the basics as you identify your target suspects. As with all things in this book, we embrace a virtual approach to the sales process. The goal is to accomplish everything from your home-based office (or without leaving your existing physical office), while sitting in your favorite chair. It's important for you to begin your sales efforts or augment current efforts with an effective suspect list to fill your virtual prospect pipeline, and master the critical basics of prospect identification. This process can be used for B2B or B2C businesses, simple sales or complex sales, local, national or even international markets.

As you review the sales tips, you may already know some of them. In these instances, you should simply skim the tip and move on to the next one. There is a logical progression with these tips; it can prove worthwhile to read through all the tips to help assimilate the overall process, and then focus on the tips that are important to your specific type of business. The sales tips in this book are organized across my 4-Phase Virtual Sales Process: **Identify, Qualify, Present** and **Close,** and assume you already have a solution you wish to sell. Phase 1 focuses on the identification of suspects who are in a designated target market and profile appropriate for your business. The following tips will help you identify your ideal prospects virtually. Your virtual prospecting must start by ensuring you're fishing in the right pond, stocked with the right type and size of fish you wish to catch.

Tip 1 Put Your Car Keys on Your Desk and Leave Them There

Resist the urge to put on the suit and tie, grab your keys, get in your car and drive 30 minutes to meet with a prospect face to face. Web based selling is more efficient, more profitable and if done correctly, more effective than the traditional road warrior mentality. As you review the selling techniques and methods in this book, remember that it all begins with less time on the road and more time closing business through web based selling.

Tip 2 Determine Your Target Market and Build a Great Suspect List

Many new and existing businesses fail to select the best target market(s) for their products, services and solutions, and even if they do select a great target market, they fail to create a great target prospect list. This is an important beginning and is the first step in creating a sales funnel. Spend some time ensuring you have given this step appropriate consideration. Who are your ideal buyers, what type of business, size, location and attributes are ideal for your solutions? Spend time analyzing this carefully before moving to the actual creation of your Suspect List. Once you have identified your target buyer, you need to create a target list of possible buyers, who can be reached virtually. I call this a *"suspect list."* Your initial list of targeted buyers is actually comprised of suspects (unqualified prospects), and many companies trivialize this important task. List building can be accomplished 100 percent virtually. Your suspect list, a list of targeted companies (or consumers) in your desired market, can be compiled from free sources including the fastest growing, the biggest, and the best company type lists (See the Real-World Scenario below). LinkedIn® and other social networks offer company profiles and key contacts. If the budget is available, there are many fee-based lists available on the Internet. Some of these include: D&B, Hoovers™, InfoUSA, OneSource, ZoomInfo, etc. There are append and de-duping services available from many vendors if you already have a partial list, and you should ask for emails whenever possible. We see many mature companies attempting to embark on a web selling model, hampered by a less than adequate list. If you don't have a great suspect list, a list of every contact in your target market and profile, spend the time and if possible the money, to accomplish this, and do so immediately.

 **Real-World Scenario**

When I was "selling" the manuscript of my first book, *Your Virtual Success,* I found a free list of literary agents at a site called www.1000literaryagents. com, selected my target prospects and emails and created an eMarketing campaign. I was promptly signed by an excellent agent, who sold my book to a book publisher. I came upon the literary agent site through a few simple Google searches. When I was targeting small, fast growing companies, I used the online Inc. 5000 directory, which offered detailed company information and included a link to each company's website. When I sold solutions to insurance agencies, I found many free lists of agencies available online, and many other inexpensive sources were also available. When one of our clients needed a list of trade show sponsors, we readily located a list that yielded 10,000 trade show organizers at a total cost of a few hundred dollars. Some lists are free, others are offered as a subscription-based fee for lookup. Some list providers allow you to pay by the contact for data downloads (some with and without emails) and others provide their entire list for one flat fee. It's easy to find target suspect lists online; you can also utilize associations, social networks liked LinkedIn and general Google and Bing™ searches to find target suspects. If you decide to purchase contacts, be careful when selecting your fee-based list. There are many scams out there. Research the company. Look at their website and ask about their guarantees. Get a sample of their contact information. Are the first and last names in separate columns? Do they have quality emails or do they include inappropriate emails like info@abccompany.com or sales@ xyzcompany.com. And if you utilize the emails for general e-marketing purposes, make sure you read and follow the CAN-SPAM Act or applicable guidelines for your country. Before procuring a suspect list for my company or clients, I research the source very carefully to ensure I'm working with a quality provider, and you should too.

Tip 3   Contact Management or SFA

Once you have identified your target suspects you need to deposit their contact information in some type of database. These databases are often referred to as contact management solutions or sales force automation solutions (see Appendix 1 for a definition of terms like this). Even a simple Excel type spreadsheet can act as your contact management database as you begin your marketing efforts. Cloud computing (software solutions provided over the internet requiring only a PC and Internet connection to use) contact management and sales force automation (SFA) applications such as BigContacts, ACT for Web and BatchBook are examples of inexpensive, expandable solutions that can be used by multiple users from any location. There are also PC-based applications and build-your-own Microsoft Access-type solutions that will work for many small businesses.

Salesforce.com is currently one of the industry leaders for cloud computing SFA solutions and has deep functionality. In my opinion, contact managers like BigContacts, Simple Contact and Prophet (as of this writing) are examples of contact management solutions that are often easier to use and do a better job for simple outbound prospecting than more robust SFA/customer relationship management (CRM) solutions. Cloud computing solutions typically offer 30-day trials — invest some time in your review and select a solution that is simple, easy to use and appropriate for your type of business.

In-Depth Review

Let's take a moment to review cloud computing. Though the terms may sound confusing, the concept is simple. Any entrepreneur or business can take advantage of software solutions without the need for any sophisticated computer technology at their place of business. There is no need for a server or network, just a simple PC or laptop hooked up to the Internet. These software applications run in something referred to as the "Internet cloud."

Simply put, the term *cloud* is used as a metaphor for the Internet. The cloud is in the middle of the drawing and depicts the Internet as a means to connect different computers in varied locations.

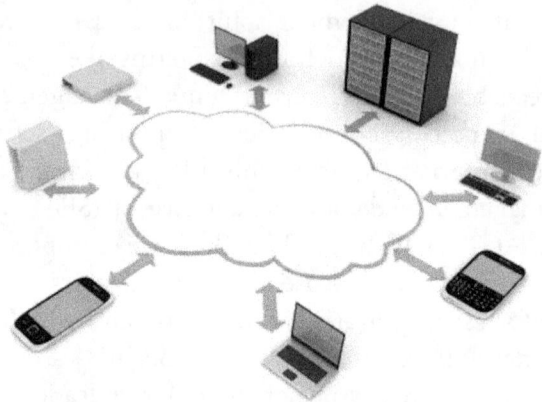

Cloud computing applications are critically important to virtual companies and web selling strategies because software solutions are sometimes free, or rented for a truly modest monthly sum, they are not purchased. Sometimes cloud computing solutions are referred to as software as a service (SaaS). Don't get confused by this, it's really the same principal, companies can utilize Web-based software like GoToMeeting, Skype or iContact without needing computer servers or a technical support staff. SaaS is frequently defined as software that is rented rather than purchased, software and applications that can be used over the internet as opposed to software which is purchased and resides on your PC. Some examples of cloud /SaaS solutions that I currently use include:

- GoToMeeting: Small Web meetings and conference call solution.

- GoToWebinar: Up to 1,000 people can attend our Web seminars.

- iContact: Email marketing solution.

- SpamCop: Filters spam and unwanted messages.

- GoDaddy.com: Hosts websites and provides email services.

- WordPress: Free blog hosting and services, can be integrated into your website.

- LinkedIn: Social networking for business.

- Skype: Free PC-to-PC calls, you can even download this to your mobile device.

Tip 4 Determine the Critical Demographics for Your Suspect Database

Though this may sound like a simple task, it's more complicated than many might think, and it's worth a little time to ensure your business is collecting actionable information. Make sure you include multiple contact names for each company, or if you're B2C, you might have multiple contacts per household, include title if applicable, and phone numbers and emails. Emails are extremely important — beware when buying email lists (follow opt-in rules) and be careful and considerate when sending emails. If you are sending individual emails, make it easy for the recipient to opt out of future emails. Aside from the traditional address and phone information, there are often many other fields available from list sources. Do you need all of these? Can you download them without creating data clutter? Are there certain mission-critical fields like revenue, employees, D&B rating, country or other demographics important to your efforts? Invest a little time and thought up front before routinely passing on data fields that may be of use in your marketing endeavors.

 **Power Tip**

Opt-in email lists are typically unavailable for purchase. Many are offered through associations and you "rent" the list with the association sending the email on your behalf. Some associations, publications and other organizations also offer newsletter sponsorships in addition to, or in place of, email blasts. Your link is included in either the email or newsletter, and you "own" the prospect emails that click through on your link or request information. The best way to attract opt-in subscribers is to create compelling content on current subjects. Some examples are: recent changes to legislation that impact your prospects, changes to regulations, improved solution functionality or efficiency, recently released models, manufacturer's price incentives or safety notifications. Web seminars, white papers, client success stories, interesting newsletters and expert speakers can help ensure your suspects become prospects and your prospects stay tuned in to your messaging.

Tip 5 Create Your Prospect Scorecard

What does your perfect client look like? Create a Prospect Scorecard to quantify your approach to prospecting and pipeline building. Some of the attributes of your ideal client might include revenue, growth rate, client type (business or consumer) and market niche. For example, are you targeting companies between $5 million and $10 million in revenue? Are your best prospects fast-growing firms like those found on the Inc. 500 list? Are you selling to consumers? If you're selling to consumers, are they high net worth prospects, middle income, younger or older? Are your prospects in a specific niche market such as banking, insurance, biotech, plumbing, consulting, education, etc.? Create a Prospect Scorecard with up to 10 ideal attributes to help you determine if you are selling to an in-profile prospect. Sample PC based and Mobile Prospect Scorecards are shown below.

PROSPECT SCORECARD - FOR B2B ORGANIZATIONS										Copyright StartUpSelling, Inc.
Prospect Attributes	ABC Co.	XYZ Co.	ones Corp	Smith Co.	Silver Co.	Sterling	USA Co.	Salt Inc.	Pepper Co	Zinc Co.
$5 to $50 Million in Revenues	1	1	1	1	1			1	1	
50+ Employees	1	1		1	1			1	1	1
Located in NY or NJ	1	1	1	1		1	1		1	1
Target Industry Vertical(s)	1	1		1	1	1		1		1
Need for Solution Like Yours	1	1	1						1	
Open to Change/New Vendors	1	1	1	1	1		1	1		1
Strong Champion/Internal Sponsor	1	1	1					1	1	
Centralized Decision Making Model	1	1	1	1				1	1	1
Previous Sale or Engagement	1	1	1	1			1	1	1	
Referral or Cross-Sale		1	1					1		
Score *	9	10	8	7	4	2	3	7	7	5
Result	Win	Win	Win	Win	Loss	Loss	Loss	Pending	Pending	Pending
* 8-10: Ideal prospect profile and a likely win | 5-7: Good prospect but be aware of out of profile attributes | 4 or under: Need a compelling reason to go after the business										
Prospect Qualifier = BUD (Capital Letter indicates that the qualifier has been validated)										
Budget	B	B	B	B	B	b	b	b	B	B
Urgency	U	U	U	U	u	u	u	u	U	u
Decision Maker	D	D	D	D	d	d	D	d	d	d

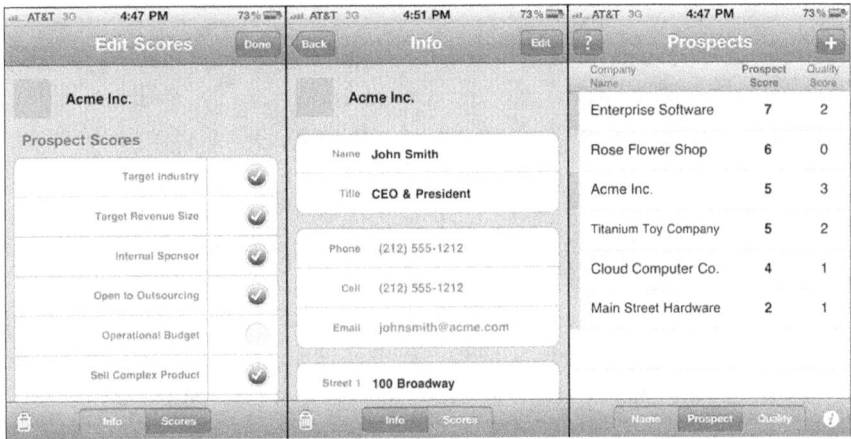

Screen 1 — **Edit Scores** / Done
Acme Inc.
Prospect Scores
- Target Industry ✓
- Target Revenue Size ✓
- Internal Sponsor ✓
- Open to Outsourcing ✓
- Operational Budget
- Sell Complex Product ✓

Info | Scores

Screen 2 — Back / **Info** / Edit
Acme Inc.
Name: John Smith
Title: CEO & President
Phone: (212) 555-1212
Cell: (212) 555-1212
Email: johnsmith@acme.com
Street 1: 100 Broadway

Info | Scores

Screen 3 — **Prospects** / +

Company Name	Prospect Score	Quality Score
Enterprise Software	7	2
Rose Flower Shop	6	0
Acme Inc.	5	3
Titanium Toy Company	5	2
Cloud Computer Co.	4	1
Main Street Hardware	2	1

Name | Prospect | Quality

Tip 6 Create Your Virtual Buyer Persona

Some organizations find it helpful to create a prospect persona. This can be a one or two paragraph written description of your ideal buyers. For example: Mike Jones is a CFO or senior financial executive who works at a company between $5 million and $50 million dollars in revenue. He's held this position at least three years and seeks to improve the systems and efficiencies within his company. He does not make quick decisions, but is willing to try new things if they have a compelling ROI. He is in the early to mid-stages of his career, and has the credibility within his organization to drive a new initiative or convince others that his decision to allocate budget is sound. He can make the decision to purchase, but may seek to validate it with other team members. Once he decides, however, the sale is very likely to move forward.

 **Power Tip**

Once you have completed your Prospect Scorecard, you can leverage your Virtual Buyer Persona and create a cutoff point to determine if your suspect is a high quality prospect. For example, if you have a prospect which is at least a 7 (out of a maximum score of 10), and has a buyer persona matching your criteria, you then know your prospect is an in profile prospect from a quantitative standpoint. If they score only a 3, they are obviously questionable. If they are a "3," it doesn't mean you can't sell them your solution but it is less likely you will do so. With limited time and resources, you want to spend time with people who can and will buy. If you are selling a very simple B2C solution over the Internet, your scorecard may only have three or four criteria. A simple survey, or a few well framed questions during the potential transaction, can help you determine who matches your criteria. Take the time to create your scorecard, it's truly worthwhile no matter what type of business you run. Often helpful is including your partners, colleagues or even friends and family in your scorecard creation process. For instance, start writing down your client's attributes on a white board or piece of paper, including industry, revenue size, employees, growth, geography, circumstances (growth, contraction, other), and the reasons they purchased. Whittle these attributes to the most important 10. Next, rank your current prospects against this profile to help you create your pipeline of "hot prospects," or you may refer to these as "pipeline worthy" prospects.

You're likely to close business when you find a high prospect score *and* a match with your buyer persona. But, how much time and effort should you expend on these tasks? An hour or two per week reviewing your prospects and pipeline is worthwhile for most entrepreneurs or small businesses.

Spending more time with those likely to buy should be your virtual credo. Virtual sales efforts are fast and efficient, refine your process and look to optimize your prospect review if you're spending more than 10 percent of your time on these types of tasks.

Tip 7 Create Your Prospect Identification Acronym (Prospect Qualifier)

At a high-growth training firm, I created the acronym called "BUD," which stands for budget, urgency and decision maker. We were likely to win the business if we had those three elements *and* were speaking with an in-profile prospect. That's why creating a Prospect Identification Acronym, which I call a "Prospect Qualifier," is critical. The Prospect Identification Acronym is placed the bottom of the Sample Prospect Scorecard (See Tip 5). In some regards, this pertains to the Virtual Qualification Phase, but it is still important to understand and leverage this concept in the Virtual Identification Phase. Create a Prospect Qualifier to help determine if the prospects identified in your scorecard are good candidates. This improves the odds of ultimately "closing the deal." An in-profile prospect, even a perfect 10 on the scorecard, doesn't mean they will buy. As you identify your target accounts, your Prospect Qualifier may qualify them out before they ever make it to the Virtual Qualification Phase. For example, if you're in the Identification Phase and you just reached the CEO but hear them say they're preparing for bankruptcy (which normally constitutes "no budget"), your suspect is unlikely to become a prospect, unless you are trying to sell bankruptcy or liquidation services.

Power Tip

Your Prospect Qualifier (qualifying acronym) will be specific to your business. Perhaps it will be BUD (budget, urgency, decision maker) or BUN (budget, urgency, need) or RENT (RFP, event, need, timing), or for complex sales something like, BUTANE (budget, urgency, timing, authority, need, event). Your Virtual Prospect Qualifier must include the key criteria you need to close a sale. For example, if you cannot close a sale without identifying a significant budget, it should be included in your Prospect Qualifier. Or, perhaps you must have a compelling hard dollar return on investment (ROI) to prove your solution can pay for itself in less than three years. Refine your Virtual Prospect Qualifier as you begin your calls. Determine which suspect attributes result in appointments and sales, then correlate these findings with both clients and prospects to create your own Prospect Qualifier. This should be a relatively fast and highly valuable exercise that will dramatically help you in the Identification and Qualification Phases of your virtual sales process. Like many aspects of your nimble virtual sales operation, your Prospect Qualifier may change over time. As you close new business, determine if there are new or different attributes about each sale.

Tip 8 Call Your Suspects to Glean Your Prospects

It's time to call your suspects to glean your prospects. A warm call is better than a cold call, and it helps to know a little bit about each suspect before calling them. Depending on your type of business, you may want to visit each and every suspect website to learn a little about them. You can quickly and easily copy company names, contacts and phone numbers into Excel and start your calling. Add rolling comments on the right-hand side of your spreadsheet, and you have an ultra-simple suspect database. You can then import your names and demographic data, along with your rolling comments into a contact management or SFA solution when you are ready.

If you have the budget, this process can be outsourced as you cull through your suspects to create a prospect list.

 **Real-World Scenario**

So where do you find a fast, cheap and easy solution to use as a contact management or SFA tool? Having spent the last 30 years running sales organizations I have more than a passing familiarity with sales force automation solutions. I've used proprietary solutions, off-the-shelf solutions, Outlook add-ons and enterprise solutions. For most salespeople who are operating independently or in a small business environment, small businesses which have not yet automated or entrepreneurs, I'd recommend a simple contact manager, SFA package or a basic database to get the job done. It must be fast and simple to use. By the way, simple is more than easy — it's easy and efficient. Most of your data should be available on one window, or two windows maximum. I can't stress this enough. If you need to navigate through five windows to note a voice mail you left and remind yourself to schedule your next call, it may be "easy," but it sure isn't fast and efficient. You will need a calendar (Outlook or an SFA Outlook compatible calendar or an SFA that integrates with your Outlook Calendar). The main functions you will need include:

- Global search: Find anything in the database (Google-type search).

- Find contact and/or find company name.

- Find contacts to call *today.*

- Next record button and previous record button.

- Hot prospect list: Generate a simple pipeline of top prospects.

- One screen repository for key data including name, phone numbers, email, demographics, notes, company background.

- Sort by key fields including state, business, and phone number.

- Record notes and call back date or next steps.

As of this writing, there are dozens of cost-effective cloud computing (Web-based) and PC-based SFA solutions to choose from including BigContacts, BatchBlue, Etolos, Saleforce.com, SalesNexus, Goldmine, Act!, Maximizer, and SalesLogix to mention just a few. Some of these are free while others can cost $50 per month or more. Select wisely, there is often a tradeoff between functionality and ease and efficiency of use. SFA systems can fail because salespeople find the solution slow and cumbersome. One of the most popular systems I used, from the sales team's perspective, was a simple one screen contact management solution created on a Microsoft Access platform. It was fast, easy, conducive to calling and following up, and it tracked all the basic information the salespeople required. Many salespeople and small businesses simply use an Excel spreadsheet for their prospecting and a separate Excel sheet for their top 10 or 20 (or more) prospects. This works fine as a starting point for many salespeople and small businesses.

Tip 9 Your Call Script Must-Haves: Top Three Differentiators

Create a succinct yet high-impact call script including your top three differentiators (we like to say "The Big 3"). If you have 10 great differentiators, you still need to cull them to three at a time, because that's the maximum number you can typically cover in any given call pitch, and arguably the most any prospect can remember during one interaction.

Your script will work best if you are specific. Remember: You know your prospects' business and need to rapidly convey this in your script. Work in your top three differentiators fast.

Here's an example of a call script our company uses:

Hi (Prospect Name) this is John Smith calling with StartUpSelling. We work with Inc. 500 companies like yours helping with lead generation and web marketing initiatives. Our CEO has been on the Inc. 500 list twice so we understand the needs of a rapidly expanding business. Our Web-based marketing methods integrate e-marketing, webinars, social media marketing and appointment setting to deliver high quality leads. And, our virtual model ensures affordable rate structures for all of our clients. Would you have any time available during the next several days for a quick web meeting? (Fallback: If they decline to meet, offer the webinar as follows.) We're also hosting a complimentary webinar on Web 2.0 marketing and using virtual sales tools, and we'd like to send you an invitation. All I need is an email address to add you to our list — would you like to attend?

In our script, we highlight our big three differentiators — our Inc. 500 background, our integrated marketing approach, and affordable rate structure. We also tell our prospects we understand Inc. 500 companies such as theirs, and we state this upfront. Next, we empathize with them by saying our CEO has been on the list twice. Finally, if our prospect declines a one-on-one meeting, we offer an alternative by asking if they would like to book a webinar.

Start by writing your script, create the branching applicable to your typical phone conversations, then practice and refine. Branches are logical, conversational and objection tangents projecting off the main trunk (or path) of your ideal outbound call. For example, in your ideal call, you connect with the decision maker, identify their needs, determine if they have budget, and set up a web meeting for continued discussion. This path has many possible variations, or branches, for both you and the prospect. List the possible objections at the end of the call script (and within logical locations in the branching). Your script will change quickly in the first few weeks as you continue to improve and refine and gain real-world experience with the phone conversations.

Succinctly record the results of every call in your suspect database. Review your results to see how your differentiators are working. Are you successfully booking appointments, and if so, what is the ratio of calls to appointments? If the numbers appear weak, try additional script refinements until you're happy with the results. Change some of your differentiators or you can even change the order each is mentioned in your script. Remember, the best scripts show an understanding of your prospect market and also rapidly explain why you can help them better than others. Rehearse your top differentiators — they should become second nature to you and your team. Use them in a wide variety of ways. We'll show you how throughout this book.

 **Power Tip**

Call Script: Be specific, let them know you know their business, and get to the Big 3 fast. Let's drill down on another version of our call script:

> *Hi (Prospect Name) this is _____ calling with StartUpSelling, we work exclusively with Insurance Agencies like yours to improve lead generation for your producers, and increase marketing reach to expand your book of business. Our Web Based Marketing methods integrate insurance agency eMarketing, webinars, social media marketing and appointment setting to deliver high quality leads. And our virtual model ensures affordable rates for agencies like yours. I'd like to offer you the opportunity to learn more about integrated insurance agency marketing in a brief online meeting. Would you have any time available during the next several days? (Fallback: If they decline to meet, offer the webinar as follows) We're also hosting a complimentary webinar on Web 2.0 Marketing and using virtual sales tools, and we'd like to send you an invitation. All I need is an email address to add you to our list – would you like to attend?*

In this sample script our big three includes our insurance agency background, our Integrated Marketing approach and affordable rate structure. We also let them know we understand insurance agencies (note the use of "producer" as opposed to salesperson and the "book of business" phrase applicable to the insurance agency industry). And we offer a webinar (lower level of commitment) if the prospect does not want a 1-1 meeting (higher level of commitment from a prospect).

Tip 10 Warm Calls, Cold Calls and Powerful Executive-to-Executive Calls

You have set your sights on your suspects and need to begin your calls. Warm calls are always easier and more effective than cold calls, though sometimes they are not possible. What's the difference? A cold call means you've had no prior contact with the suspect and are calling them for the first time, attempting to deliver your sales pitch. A warm call means you have sent them information prior to the call, or they are aware of your firm from advertising, mailings, emails, or Web seminars. Early in your process you might not have emails and your preliminary suspect calls might simply be cold calls. This is a good time to take advantage of executive-to-executive calls. For example, a senior person at your company, which can include the owner, founder or other key person, will actually make the calls.

Try beginning like this: "Hi (Prospect Name) this is John Smith, CEO of Smith Company, and I'm making some senior level calls today to determine the best approach to assist (work with/meet with/further discussions) your company..." Some refer to this as level matching, but regardless of the label, executives prefer dealing with senior level associates whenever possible.

Tip 11 Voice Mail Pitches

When calling, it's best to engage prospects in a real time discussion. However, for some solutions, voice mails might be used early and often, while for other types of businesses, voice mails are only used after multiple attempts have failed to result in a real-time call. Your business should have multiple voice mail pitches, focusing on your top 10 differentiators. For example, try creating five different voice mail pitches featuring two key differentiators. You *must* try different and compelling voice mails when leaving a voice mail message. The voice mails should be slightly different, touching on different "hot buttons" but revolving around your central theme (Remember: Use the Big 3 differentiators). Don't forget to show enthusiasm and expertise in your real-time calls and voice mail pitches.

 **Power Tip**

Let's review some differentiators. At StartUpSelling, Inc., we focus our pitches vertically and then highlight our areas of expertise. For example, if we are prospecting in the insurance agency vertical, we mention our proficiency in property and casualty, benefits, commercial or transportation, and how our marketing solutions have helped each specific area. Our pitch would be, "Hi this is Alan Smith calling on behalf of StartUpSelling. We work with benefits agencies like yours to help increase their book of business through targeted e-marketing and Web seminar marketing campaigns. Recently, we attracted over 100 HR executives to a Web seminar focused on recent COBRA changes. Have you thought about improving agency lead generation using e-marketing and webinars?"

There are numerous differentiators listed above. Terms like "benefits agencies," "book of business," "HR executives" and "COBRA," help us show our familiarity with the industry. Simultaneously, we note our expertise in Web seminar marketing. This pitch could be changed easily by focusing on outsourced appointment setting, client testimonials, social media marketing, website improvements, etc. The key to both real time and voice mail pitches, is to keep them relevant, short and varied, while maintaining a constant theme. The same type of information can and should be used in other marketing mediums including website content, blogs, e-published articles, e-marketing, etc.

Tip 12 Transfer Enthusiasm Using Voice Inflection and Cadence

Have you ever listened to a boring, monotone documentary that a teacher insisted would be educational? It probably wasn't very elucidating because it was uninteresting and dull. The same issue is true for your prospecting calls and, as you will learn later, your virtual presentations. Instill enthusiasm through voice cadence and inflection. If you're excited about your solution, transfer that feeling to your prospects. If you're not excited about your solution, go back to Step 1 and find a solution you're excited about and can sell and market virtually.

Tip 13   Get Emails Whenever Possible!

When you're making your calls, find a reason to elicit your prospect's email address. Offer to send a case study, white paper, newsletter or webinar invitation in exchange for their basic contact information and email. This will help you build your email list, a critical component in your virtual sales and marketing efforts.

⚡ Watch-Out Tip

When using emails make sure you never "spam" your prospective clients. You should follow CAN-SPAM regulations (or regulations pertaining to the countries in which you are selling) and use common sense e-marketing best practices. When building your opt-in list, leverage educational offers, such as a Web seminar on an educational topic, a newsletter or white paper. Always offer an easy and obvious opt-out link, and never try to "sell" in your early email interactions.

Tip 14   Determine Need: Learn Your Prospect's Solution Requirements

What are you selling? How does it fit your prospective client's needs? If they say they never outsource (or would never use your type of solution), and they have a definitive reason, move on. They will not progress to the Qualify Phase. Do they need accounting services, lead generation, lawn care, landscaping, marketing consulting or carpentry? Are their specific requirements a good match for your solution? Do they have certain standards, tolerances, methodologies or cultural requirements which are conducive to a sale, or should you dismiss this prospect and move on to better opportunities? No matter what your prospect market is, you need to understand its specific requirements and ensure your solution meets its specific needs, both today and in the future.

Tip 15　Call and Email High

The ultimate goal is to identify the decision maker and pitch your solution directly to them. This may seem easier than it really is, because the decision maker can vary in every organization. In some cases, it can be a CEO, COO or CFO, in others the vice president of sales, vice president of marketing, or vice president of customer service. In larger organizations it can be a manager, and in smaller organizations decisions often require owner approval. Committee decisions are always challenging, whereby a committee makes a recommendation that is then presented to the decision maker. Even in simpler B2C sales it can be difficult to determine which family member(s) makes the final decision for a home purchase, whether it is a new roof, new hardwood floors, or a $75,000 addition. It's very important to determine the decision maker as early in the process as possible. After all, you can create a lot of work with no results if the decision maker has already made up their mind to use a different provider.

Tip 16　Call and Email Wide

Calling "wide" is very important for most types of solution sales. Depending upon your type of B2B sale, you may need to call two people (or, two titles), or 22 people if you are in a large and complex enterprise sale. Though large procurement decisions are often made by a senior manager or vice president, sign-off or final buy-in often occurs at a higher level, sometimes with the CEO, or owner if privately held. By calling wide, you accomplish two very important tasks — you determine the key influencers in the process, and you can determine who makes the final decision. Don't be surprised, however, if you need a "head nod" from multiple executives to receive final sign-off from the decision maker if you are in a complex sales process. Calling wide is particularly important in the virtual sale because you will not meet with these prospects face to face, and you must deduce the political landscape from calls and Web meetings.

In-Depth Review

Imagine an executive team sitting around a long conference room table, discussing their business opportunities and challenges. Perhaps there are three or four executives in a smaller company, and 10 or more in a larger company. Who would attend this type of meeting? A CEO, CFO, CTO and CMO might be likely "C-level" titles. For certain types of companies, you might find a general manager, vice president of sales, vice president of customer service, vice president of manufacturing, president, vice president of human resources, director of quality control, and so on. Now, imagine a discussion about the company's lead generation strategy, branding initiative, new website, upcoming marketing campaign, personnel shortage, product transit challenge, supplier shortage or other issues or initiatives that might be discussed. Let's say the discussion turns to a new website initiative, one which would include new blogs, video, dynamic content, and a new logo. The CMO turns to the vice president of sales and says, "Yesterday I got a phone call and an email from a company called StartUpSelling about their website video services." The vice president nods and says, "So did I." The CEO, CFO and vice president of customer service chuckle and say they were all contacted yesterday, too. This is a great example of calling (and emailing) high *and* wide. Depending on the solution your company offers, and the prospect target size, you need to identify and contact all of the possible decision makers and key influencers who can help you advance in the sales cycle. Next time there is an executive team meeting at one of your prospective clients, make your company one of the topics on their list.

Tip 17 Take Advantage of the 'Virtual Push-Down Effect'

Contact the CEO and other C-level executives. Concisely explain what you do and try to secure a web meeting. Often they (or their executive assistant) may direct you to another individual who handles your type of solution for their company. When calling that vice president or manager-level contact, make certain you mention the CEO (or other important name and title) suggested you call them. Watch how fast your calls are returned when you've been pushed down and use this method to contact the vice president-level key influencers and decision makers. Calling high can often help your efforts to call wide.

 **Real-World Scenario**

About ten years ago, I helped a company develop their virtual sales and marketing strategy. Its solution, let's describe it as a client behavioral research solution, was new to the market and required an evangelical sale. The businesses targeted for this new solution had to be convinced to take a leap of faith and try a new method to analyze their customer behavior. In addition, this method was a completely Web-based, SaaS solution. Evangelical sales are common with technology companies seeking to sell a breakthrough product (e.g., eMarketing solutions, MP3 downloads, cloud computing, electronic reading devices, and even DVRs). The first step in the process was to identify the target market and build a suspect list, just as I mentioned above. The CEO had an insurance background and landed a few insurance company clients. We decided this would be the first niche market to target. How did we build a comprehensive virtual suspect list? We utilized several top 100 industry lists and imported them into a simple Microsoft database. We searched for on-line insurance company listings and added them to our virtual suspect list. Then, we called every one of these insurance organizations (there were about 300 initially targeted). These targeted cold calls resulted in up-to-date contact information, key executives, titles, direct phone numbers, and emails. These were often gathered by offering the suspects an opportunity to attend an informational Web seminar. Within a few short months, the database was quite comprehensive, and the suspect list began to yield a compelling prospect list. Utilizing my Prospect Scorecard system and qualifying acronym, we were able to identify possible buyers, convince these buyers to review the solution in a Web seminar or one-to-one web meeting, and then move them to the qualification phase. Out of the 300 initial suspects targeted, we were able to convince over 150 to review the solution in our first year of sales efforts, and about 20 percent of them purchased within that same year. An impressive result for a self-funded, emerging operation selling 99 percent virtually, without travel or face-to-face meetings and the costs and inefficiencies associated with that model. Today, many years after we helped this client create a target suspect list, they continue to dominate their niche.

Tip 18 Determine the Decision Maker and the Decision Making Process

When reaching out to target suspects, determining the decision maker is often difficult during the identification phase. However, determining the decision making process is often much easier. For example, let's say you identify a high quality suspect, and consider them to be a likely prospect. You can then ask a very important and elucidating question, "If your company decided to purchase a solution like this, what would the process look like, and who might get involved?" This relatively short question can be asked multiple times throughout the 4-Phase Virtual Sales Process. It acts as a beacon, helping you better identify, qualify and navigate the balance of your sales process. It's important to understand every intricacy in the decision making process so you know what can go right and what could go wrong, helping ensure you improve the likelihood of a successful outcome.

Tip 19   Avoiding 'Maybe'

As we move from the virtual identify phase to the virtual qualify phase, we begin to cull our suspects into prospects. This begins as soon as we pick up the phone, and suspects self-qualify out of your prospect pool. They may be preparing to be acquired, filing for Chapter 11 bankruptcy, or just purchased a solution like yours. This is great news; they are a firm "No." They are not prospects and are unlikely to be for some time. It's really important that you cull out suspects. If you're unable to do this during the identify phase, it's even more important to accomplish this in the qualify phase. We often say that "Yes" is good. "No" is good. But, "maybe" will kill you because in your virtual sales pipeline every "maybe" that doesn't buy from you creates a large opportunity cost. You have limited time and resources and must spend them wisely. Although salespeople never want to hear "no," it's really the "maybe" that can be costly.

Tip 20   Leverage Social Networking to Gain Key Contact Information

When seeking virtual prospect opportunities, don't underestimate the power of networking, including social networks, to provide access to key decision makers in your target accounts. Traditional networking can be done virtually via telephone, Skype, Web meetings and email. And, of course, it can be done face to face, through local networking organizations. Online social networks, however, offer much greater reach. For example, LinkedIn has well over 100 million members as of this writing. Millions of contacts are available for you to glean key contact information and establish connections.

We've now reviewed the top 20 tips in the Virtual Identification Phase, so let's move on to the web sales tips designed to help you better qualify your prospects and separate buyers from lookers.

Chapter 2

Phase 2: Qualify

Chapter 2 reviews the qualification phase of the 4-Phase Virtual Sales Process. Superior qualification skills are extremely important in the virtual sales process. Depending on your type of business, leveraging Skype-type technology and video-enabled Web meeting solutions will afford you the opportunity to meet and see your prospects, though your ability to sense body language is more limited than on-site meetings. Many Web meeting technologies incorporate audio and allow document sharing, but some do not provide video. In these cases, verbal clues and focused questions become instrumental in successful qualification. Since the physical interaction and nuances are limited, you must use all your "web" senses to compensate. This chapter will help you learn how to create your own virtual qualification process, ask the hard qualifying questions, listen for virtual qualification clues from the prospect, and gauge the authority of your internal champion to determine the relative quality of the opportunity. Superior virtual qualification will lead to a more effective close ratio, and thus, a more efficient and profitable business.

Tip 21 Complete Your Prospect Scorecard for Worthy Prospects

The Prospect Scorecard was mentioned in Tip 5 and Tip 7. In the qualification phase, it's time to score each prospect using the Prospect Scorecard criteria you created. As you work with each of your prospects, quickly determine where they rank on your scale. For example, if you're using a 5-point scale and your prospect ranks a "4" out of "5" on that scale, they are a worthy time investment for your business. If they only rank a "1" out of "5," they should not be on your sales pipeline unless there is an extraordinary reason.

Scrutinize the opportunity to determine if they should be considered a pipeline prospect. If they are a long shot, why are you investing your time and energy in this particular opportunity? Remember, you should be spending time with people who are likely to buy. Make sure the top of your pipeline is a reasonable and workable number. For many sales professionals this might be five to 15 prospects. If you have 50 prospects at the top of your pipeline, it will likely be an unworkable number as you fail to offer sufficient attention to each to secure an order. Obviously, this will change based on the selling price of your solution. If you're selling custom hats, you will need more prospects than if you're selling solutions that cost $20,000 or more. See the next Power Tip for further details on how to create and use a Prospect Scorecard. Go to: http://www.ProspectScorecard.com to see a sample Prospect Scorecard (or to learn about the Prospect Scorecard Mobile App). Or you can use the sample in this book's Appendix 2.

 **Power Tip**

Let's examine how to create and use your Prospect Scorecard. What are the attributes of your best clients? What do they have in common? In what ways are their businesses, activities, methodologies, products, services or approach to the market similar? If you were to create a list of five or 10 attributes about each of them, which would be the most common among them? For example, let's say you are a small marketing services firm selling

Web-based marketing services to small businesses. What are the most likely attributes you might find among your clients? Perhaps they are:

1. Open to outsourcing marketing.

2. Annual revenues between $1 million and $10 million.

3. Located in North America.

4. B2B product, service or solution offering.

5. Considered purchase solution (not a commodity) priced at $1,000 or higher.

6. Small internal marketing department, or limited Web 2.0 marketing resources.

This is a good start. We have now identified six common attributes across your client base. Do these make sense? Do your preferred clients fit within the profile above? If so, you can create a 6-point scale for your ideal client profile, measuring prospects from a quantitative standpoint against this attribute list. Once this has been established, you can create a metric to determine if your prospect pool or pipeline contains in-profile prospects. In the example above, you might deem any prospect scoring a "4" or more out of "6" to be a good prospect, and any prospect "3" or below to be a low quality prospect. Of course, if you have a "6," or a prospect who has all of your attributes, you have a prospect which is 100 percent in-profile and worthy of your time and resource investment as you move forward in your sales process.

Tip 22 Ask the Hard Questions: Begin This Process Early

What are the hard questions? Depending upon your type of business, some examples might include:

- Has the individual with whom you're conversing ever made a purchase like this before?

- How many levels of approval are needed for this type of purchase?

- Which budget will be used and who is the budget holder?

- Is there a formal procurement process?

- Who signs the order? (Will you be the one placing the order?)

- When is the deadline for implementation (or purchase)?

Tip 23 If Asked Correctly, the Hard Questions Aren't Very Hard

These types of insightful questions cannot be asked all at once. You need to develop a rapport to glean answers without annoying your prospective client or appearing overly assertive. Often, a lead-in question such as, "Do you mind if I ask you a few process-related questions before we move on?" can yield great results in a B2B sale. In a B2C sale, something as simple as "Will this order be shipped to you or is it a gift to be shipped to a different address?" is one of many effective questions you can ask. This can be done in-person, over the phone, or in a Web meeting. It can be done in almost any sales process, simple or complex. I've asked these questions in many types of sales situations, and have also heard them when placing a simple order at Lands' End. Conversely, I've made many large-scale purchases where sales executives consistently fail to ask these types of questions.

Tip 24 Determine Pain Points

Often, our top priority is to mitigate the pain, whether we're talking about personal health or the health of our business. If your solution addresses an important issue, specifically a pain point which your prospect needs and wants to address, you are much more likely to close the business. For example, if your solution generates leads, and your prospect is experiencing a dip in their sales and pipeline activity, your solution addresses that specific pain point. Or, if your transportation accounting software or service automatically generates "hours of service" records for 1099 owner operators, and this is a current issue for your prospect, once again, you have mitigated the pain. Lastly, and perhaps more simply, if your pest removal services can eliminate a hornet, wasp or bee infestation, one in which a prospective client experienced a recent sting, then you figuratively, and literally, have addressed a pain point.

Tip 25 Gauge Your Sponsor/ Champion's Authority

In a more complex sale, one in which you are removed from the final decision maker, it's important to determine the authority level of your internal champion, also referred by some as your sponsor. Have they been with the company long? Have they made a buying decision like this before? Do they bring the recommendation to the owner, the CEO or some other final decision maker? Do they know this person well? These are a few of the important questions you need to determine, to gauge your champion's authority level and better qualify your opportunity.

 **Power Tip**

Let's review how to evaluate your internal champion or sponsor. For complex sales and sales to larger organizations, it's essential to thoroughly evaluate your internal champion (also referred to a "key influencer" or "internal advocate"). With limited time, money and resources, it's imperative that you invest your time with people who can buy. When dealing with a sponsor, you're at least one step removed from the decision maker, who can be a CEO, CFO, vice president or even a committee. In some sales cycles you may be shielded from the decision maker, never actually able to meet with them. And you don't want to invest hours, days or weeks of cycles with someone who is destined to be rejected by the final decision maker. How can you evaluate your sponsor? Tip 22 reviewed some of the hard questions you need to ask to determine the likelihood of a purchase. You need to determine:

- If a budget is established.

- The internal process for that prospect to execute the order, which I refer to as the "Path to Purchase," or P2P.

- The authority level of your sponsor.

- If you're dealing with a want or a need (company initiative).

- If your sponsor is a seasoned veteran or new to the company.

- Who signs the agreement?

- How this purchase ranks on their comfort-level scale, is it a large procurement, a leading edge solution, or rather typical for your prospect.

For example, a $10 million company can make a $5,000 purchase without much scrutiny, but will look very closely at a $150,000 purchase. A new technology requiring extensive training or change management can be much harder to sell than a commodity-based product that must be purchased from someone. For complex or larger sales where you're working with a sponsor, the efficacy of this individual will usually determine the ultimate success of your virtual sales cycle.

Tip 26   Develop Virtual Rapport

Building rapport is just as important today as it was 50 years ago, and can be accomplished virtually and successfully. As we move to a more virtual sales and marketing approach, new tools empower our ability to build rapport with prospects utilizing both telephony and Web-centric methods. Today, many of my business "calls" with prospects and clients are done on Skype and almost all of our contractor calls are done "face-to-face" using Skype video calling. These PC-to-PC calls are currently free, and for a modest fee you can do multiparty video calls, an impressive way to have prospects meet you and your small team. Of course, building rapport can be done by phone and using Web meeting tools, including those from Citrix, Microsoft, Adobe, and many more (many of these Web meeting tools are now integrating video). Progressively more interactions and transactions are now done over the Web. At StartUpSelling, Inc., and StartMarketingTech.com, 99 percent of our project engagements are done virtually, never meeting with the client in person. Resist temptation, don't get into your car and drive 15 miles to that appointment. Leverage Skype, Web meeting tools and traditional telephony to build rapport and close business. You don't have to meet someone in person to establish credibility and trust. Remember Tip #1, put your car keys on your desk and leave them there.

 ## Real-World Scenario

Let's examine visual and verbal clues for building rapport. Several years ago, I helped a sales person virtually qualify a prospect using conference calls, email and a simple PowerPoint presentation, which then culminated in an on-site meeting with our corporate sponsor (champion) and his senior vice president. The challenge was a stalled pipeline prospect and the sales manager didn't know why. The internal sponsor knew that a decision on the project would ultimately need to be made, but kept asking for more information, resulting in a complete standstill in the sales process. I suggested we have a conference call with this sponsor, hoping to elicit some clues, improve rapport and find a catalyst to move the process forward.

The prospect was interested enough to take the call, though his availability suggested he was not at the highest executive level since he could make himself available at a moment's notice. This is not guaranteed to be an accurate assessment of responsibility, but a good clue. We mapped out a plan for the call, which included process-related questions to determine if and how a purchase could be made. After the introductions had been made and we bantered about the weather, I said, "It seems you're very interested in creating a custom training program to roll out your new software and we know the deadline is closing in. Why haven't you made a decision yet? Is there a logistical issue internally?" These questions, which some salespeople find difficult to ask, are necessary to elicit direct feedback around internal decision making, political issues and the pending purchase process. The sponsor responded that he was interested in a customized training rollout, was feeling pressure to do something but could not convince his boss, a senior VP, to take the time to decide on a solution or vendor. You could hear the frustration in his voice and the trepidation about the project, as he felt tasked with the responsibility of the rollout, yet was powerless to get something done.

I offered a solution, something which we discussed as a team when we mapped out our call plan. "We can provide a complimentary two-hour consultation with you and your senior vice president, which can start with a 10-minute conference call and culminate with advice on a rollout plan in your New York offices. The consultation has no obligation and both you and the SVP will learn about the new technologies available for these types of rollouts," I explained. The sponsor jumped at this offer, arranged a conference call with his senior vice president a few days later (to ensure he was the decision maker), which then resulted in an onsite meeting. The sale closed quickly, after a one hour on-site meeting, which today could easily be done via a Web meeting.

Virtual clues can be found throughout the process by analyzing behavior, listening to the voice cadence, gauging the authority level, determining the process, asking the hard questions. These clues will help solve the puzzle and close the deal.

Tip 27   Determine Your Path to Purchase (P2P) Steps

Every sales cycle has a P2P, an ideal path to purchase. Some are very simple, others more complex. Create a standard Path to Purchase for your solution, then track your progress by monitoring the specifics for any given prospect. For example, if your solutions require a five-step process which includes (1) an initial call, (2) then qualifying questions, (3) a Web presentation, (4) a proposal, and (5) a closing call, then you have identified a basic path to track your progress.

 **In-Depth Review**

A P2P is not the same as your 4-Phase Virtual Sales Process – it's actually a subset or microcosm of your overall process. Every sales cycle benefits from the determination of a general, sequential path. Yes there will be many small streets and alleys branching off your path, but your goal should always be to return to your standard, fundamental Path to Purchase. Here's a sample P2P. Your version might be simpler or more complex.

1. Prospect is qualified and has a well-defined need.

2. They are a "7" or higher on your Prospect Scorecard (or appropriate based on your qualification metric).

3. You have qualified the prospect, identified a decision maker and there is a clear sense of urgency to implement your solution.

4. You have set up a Web presentation and invited key participants.

5. You have gleaned important information from your internal sponsor and understand what needs to be presented at the Web meeting.

6. This is a budgeted initiative, and you have discussed the type of investment needed for your solution. Your internal sponsor said you were "in the ballpark." But you will qualify further.

7. You intend to set up a personal Web meeting with your sponsor and the decision maker after your next group Web presentation.

8. You will create a proposal after your executive meeting, and set up a review.

9. You have created a timeline to understand how and when your solution needs to be purchased and implemented.

10. You are learning about their procurement process and determine the most effective way to finalize your sale.

Tip 28 Determine Appropriate Product/Service/Solution

Let's say you offer five types of solutions. Which one is best for your prospective client? Which one are they most likely to purchase? There are many nuances to these statements. For example, perhaps they really want a full-blown sales coaching engagement which costs $5,000 per month. Is that the best solution for them? Is there sufficient budget for approval? Should you pitch a paid project pilot instead of a full blown purchase? As your qualification progresses, ask questions and strategize on the best solution or solution mix for both your client and your sales cycle.

Tip 29 Use the 1/10th of 1 Percent Sales Price Rule or Create Your Own

Let's say you're selling a survey research service costing $10,000. Does the dollar amount represent a small or large investment for your prospects? One way to answer the question is to use the 1/10th of 1 percent rule. I created this metric for many of the solutions I represented over the years and it was both simple and helpful. If your company is trying to sell a $10,000 solution to a prospect which has $1 million in annual revenues, your solution would cost them 1 percent of their revenues. That's a fairly significant number to them, one which is likely to require scrutiny, perhaps requiring the CEO to sign off on the purchase. However, if you're selling the same solution to a $25 million company, the purchase is well under 1/10th of 1 percent and would likely be under the radar — often requiring departmental approval and fitting within existing budget amounts. Further, if the purchase is well under 1/10th of 1 percent the prospect might be able to leverage operational budget money, often a faster and easier path than a capital purchase. The same rule holds true for B2C sales, find a working ratio between the investment for your solution and the target household income.

 **Power Tip**

Do not underestimate the importance of your selling price to revenue ratio (SPR), or selling price to household income of your prospect (SPI). As mentioned in Tip 29, your selling price needs to comfortably match your prospect's revenue or income level to maximize your close ratio. If you're selling residential landscape design, you might need to target affluent towns and neighborhoods. If your services start at $12,000, for example, you might need to target an area with household incomes averaging at least $150,000. If you're selling software solutions that start at $50,000, you need to determine the lowest entry-level revenue that will support that type of purchase. Using the 1/10th of 1 percent rule for your SPR, you might target companies with revenues greater than $50 million, if your solution costs $50,000. Could a company with $25 million in revenues afford your solution? It's certainly possible they could although the purchase will probably require a greater degree of scrutiny. Spend some time determining how successful you are closing deals at the lower and higher end of your prospect revenue profile to determine your ideal SPR.

Tip 30 Determine Necessary Participants for Your Presentation or Pitch

This tip is crucial for both B2B and B2C sales. What are you selling and who needs to see it to purchase? If you're selling kitchen and bath renovation, it's likely you want both/all the homeowners to be present to better qualify the likelihood of your sale. If one spouse loves your kitchen renovation plan, but you learn the other spouse thinks it is much too expensive, the likelihood of your sale drops significantly. For complex sales requiring large investments such as software solutions or technology acquisitions, make sure all key influencers, the decision maker, and the budget holder are present, or at a minimum, find a way to interact with them. We've seen sales cycles where the budget holder had to be "sold" at the very end of the process. The key influencers were unaware the budget holder wanted direct involvement in the presentation of the solution or service. Make sure you understand the P2P for each sales opportunity, and both you and your prospects are aware of the nuances of the path to optimize your close ratio.

Tip 31   Create a Reverse Timeline

Over 20 years ago, I created something I refer to as the Reverse (or backward) Timeline. This is an extremely valuable sales tool for any project-oriented, process-oriented or time-sensitive sale. The Reverse Timeline begins when you write down the rollout date, or delivery date, provided by your prospect and work backwards through the necessary steps for completion right up to today. This can help instill urgency into any sales cycle without being pushy or overbearing. Remember, if it's their deadline, it's their job, reputation or bonus at stake.

 **Power Tip**

Use a Reverse Timeline to demonstrate your knowledge of the prospect's industry and instill urgency into the decision-making process. In the Sample Reverse Timeline below, note how close the May 1 date and action item regarding contract execution are to the date of "Today!"

Sample Reverse Timeline for a Training Project Rollout

September 1	**Project deadline: Project must go live**
August 15	Deadline: End-user training must be completed
August 8	End-user training initiated
July 28	Prototype training tested in multiple locations

July 25	Customized training program and materials finalized
July 10	List of employees to be trained is finalized
July 5	Training dates selected and published
June 30	Prototype training program and materials created
June 17	Training plan submitted for review
May 10	Project Kickoff: Plan discussion and needs analysis
May 1	**Agreement must be signed to meet project deadline**
April 20	Today!

In-Depth Review

For many solutions, the Reverse Timeline is an extremely powerful qualifying and closing tool. It can be used to motivate your prospective buyer and to create or heighten urgency. I often leverage Reverse Timelines to illustrate the decision-making process in time sensitive projects or deliveries for the prospective buyer. For example, if your prospect wishes to have their house and yard in pristine shape for a wedding in June, this can be leveraged to instill urgency for a rapid decision without making the prospective client feel like you're pressuring them. If a company needs to roll out a new accounting system, and has a completion date of December 30, you can present a Reverse Timeline to them in September to demonstrate you understand the process, and instill urgency into the purchasing decision. Reverse Timelines can be done in PowerPoint for a Web meeting, on a Word Document (in advance of an on-site meeting), on a PC flowchart, or on a white board (on-site or virtual). When you're asking the prospect for input (dates, deadlines, and goals), real-time presentations can result in a collaborative and highly effective process. You should be well versed and rehearsed when it comes to your typical Reverse Timeline to impress your prospective clients with your industry knowledge and the understanding of how this knowledge relates to their specific deliverable requirements.

Tip 32   Offer ROI Assistance

In some cases, prospective clients have already determined their return on investment (ROI) which is why they intend to make a purchase in the first place. Perhaps a prospect is considering new windows for their home or business and there is a tax credit and annual fuel savings they anticipate. They may have already calculated an ROI from their own research. If not, you should provide a clear and simple ROI calculation to ensure they understand why your solution offers compelling value. The same ROI methods can work for simple value propositions and complex solution sales, such as software and technology solutions. Make sure you spend time discussing and demonstrating ROI as part of your qualification process. Create a simple one-page ROI overview, a client case study or you can offer an online calculator on your website. The ROI information can help you navigate sales opportunities when you are working with an internal sponsor or committee, helping the ultimate decision maker move forward with a compelling and verifiable ROI. Remember, there are both hard and soft ROIs, though in most instances a hard ROI works best.

 **Power Tip**

Create a compelling ROI scenario for your prospects. Suppose you have an in-profile prospect who is interested in your solution. The prospect asked for a presentation to their team. However, the prospect acknowledged they are unbudgeted and warned they may not be able to purchase your solution unless they can convince "upper management." (Don't forget to ask what titles and names "upper management" refers to.) What should you do? Leverage your ROI collateral and scenarios. Many products, services and solutions offer a hard or soft ROI — or both. For example, lawn services reduce the time needed to maintain your lawn (soft ROI) and increase the value of your home by $x\%$ (hard ROI). If you offer lead generation services, your ROI calculations might show you can add $x\%$ more leads to your pipeline, which at your current close ratio will increase your sales by an expected $y\%$ (hard ROI). Solar panels will reduce your costs of electricity by $x\%$, provide a tax rebate of y dollars, and pay for themselves in z years to save $x\%$ in costs over a 10 year period (hard ROI), and help reduce your energy footprint (soft ROI). Make sure you have compelling collateral for your ROI discussion, real life case studies, written client testimonials or client video testimonials (including recorded Skype video interviews) and a public or private website calculator if and when possible.

Tip 33　Find Out If the Initiative Is Budgeted

In Tip 13, we discussed your Prospect Scorecard (go to www. ProspectScorecard.com for more information) that includes a qualifier acronym to determine if your prospect is likely to buy. One of the examples offered was BUD, which in this case stands for budget, urgency and decision maker. Let's discuss what budget really means to your sales qualification process. Without a budget, a clearly defined need is often downgraded to a simple want. In other words, although my kitchen looks dated and I determine I need a new one, if I don't have the tens of thousands of dollars necessary (or I'm unwilling to finance that amount), it's merely a "want," not a "need." On a more sophisticated scale, if a company needs to improve its solution offering and wishes to run a comprehensive series of focus groups, but does not have budget for the initiative, then the focus group is again a want — it's something a company would like to do, but cannot because there is no budget available. Ask the hard questions early in your process to determine if budget is available or will be made available, or review your ROI scenarios with your internal sponsor to determine if an ROI driven value proposition would be a sufficient catalyst to create budget for your solution.

Tip 34　Alternative Ways to Purchase If Adequate Budget Is Not Available?

Many options are available to help prospects purchase when they are unable to find sufficient capital. Rental programs, lease programs, lease purchase, pilot to purchase, and crossing payments over two fiscal years are all options to consider. You could allow them to mix payment methods, some portion via credit card, some cash, and your own internal financing option. If your business model allows, you can create a lease purchase with a balloon payment; however, be cautious with this plan as it carries associated risk. If your sale is profitable without the balloon, your risks are obviously mitigated. Try coordinating special terms with leasing companies or banks to make it better, faster and easier for your prospects to purchase. In addition, you can offer a "lite" version of your solution, and then upgrade the client at a later date. Some companies offer *capital* budgets for one component of the purchase (e.g., hardware) and *operational* budgets for the installation and training — two different budget buckets, which might help your prospects better afford the investment. Examine all available options and be ready to provide your best prospects with alternative methods to buy your solution.

Tip 35　Determine If There Is a Formal Procurement Process

Larger and more expensive solutions often require many people to participate in the decision making process and are typically considered purchases (rather than impulse or inexpensive commodity purchases). When selling such solutions, it's reasonable to assume the organization will have a purchasing department, or at a minimum, a formal procurement process. Identify all the steps and individuals (or titles) involved in that process. Are multiple bids required? If the purchase exceeds a certain dollar amount, are additional signatures required? Does the purchasing department or process require you become an authorized vendor, or are they required to contact authorized vendors if your solution or service is similar to a preferred vendor? Do they have special provisions to purchase from small or local businesses? Can this help or hurt your efforts? Make sure you perform the requisite due diligence around the procurement process before moving too deeply in your sales process.

 **Power Tip**

Don't assume your internal sponsor understands their own internal procurement process. Ask specific, hypothetical questions to determine their knowledge of procurement. Does their process include a legal review cycle, and if so, could this adversely impact delivery? Do they require that you must use their boilerplate contract? Do they need to review the financial viability of your company? Do they need to create a formal RFP (Request for Proposal) or RFI (Request for Information) before a purchase can be consummated? Ensure your sponsor understands the procurement process, and if either of you is uncertain, ask the questions noted in Tip 35 to find out the P2P details.

Tip 36   Get Past Legal Hurdles

During the closing phase, you may encounter challenges with your prospect's lawyer or legal department. In some cases, if you have your own legal department, the challenge might actually be your own legal requirements. But for now, let's focus on a few important qualifying questions for the legal department. Do they have a lawyer or legal department that must review your contract? Do they insist on using their own contract? How long does it take to review a typical purchase? Can you work with them directly or does your sponsor act as the liaison? Do they insist on certain standard clauses, which must be included in every contract, and if so, can your sponsor provide those for you to review? Is your solution considered a work for hire, do they require ownership of IP, are there onerous damages clauses? Will they consider a mandatory arbitration clause which might be helpful to your boutique operation? We don't want to get too far ahead of ourselves in the sales process, but it's helpful to identify potential issues early and to have a game plan to solve them in the present and close phases. Though many of these questions pertain to B2B sales, some are also relevant for B2C sales. If you can simplify your own contract, it can help reduce the legal hurdles immensely. Consider creating an order form with the key legal clauses you require on the back of the form or on page two and include an arbitration clause. Simpler is usually better. If you wind up in a legal battle before or after the sale, it's usually a losing proposition for everyone.

Tip 37 Determine If There Is a Special Budget Threshold

Let's say your prospect has a policy where all orders over $10,000 need two signatures and all orders over $100,000 require CFO approval and formal sign off. As you continually seek to simplify your sales process, you are keenly aware that you would be more efficient with one signature and an initial sale of $9,000 rather than a more complex and logistically challenging $10,000 sale. Always ask your internal sponsor to check on these budget and purchase policies prior to submitting your final agreement for signature.

 **Watch-Out Tip**

Be wary of prospects who shrug off purchase-related questions with nonchalant responses, simply stating they have the authority to buy. There is a strong likelihood they will have to involve others even though they may have authority to buy. For example, look at large household purchases for windows, painting, kitchen cabinets, or counters, etc. If there are two homeowners, both will probably need to attend your presentation before a purchasing decision will be made. In the corporate world, it's unlikely one manager can decide to purchase a $100,000 item without approval at the vice president level. The more expensive the purchase, the more likely multiple layers of management and other formal processes will be encountered.

Tip 38   Operational vs. Capital Budgets and Lease vs. Purchase

Structure sales in the easiest ways to help your prospects make a purchase. Operational budgets for businesses are often easier to tap than capital budgets because they typically require fewer hurdles for approval, allowing directors and managers to use their best discretion for purchasing or renting solutions and services. For B2C sales, rentals or leases often offer an easier P2P when compared to outright purchase. If you want to offer credit card purchases, a simple way to do this is through PayPal if your volume is low or through the many options with ecommerce sites. During the qualification phase, determine if your prospect has a preference should they wish to purchase. This will also help you better gauge their level of interest.

Tip 39   Determine the Final Signatory

Who signs the contract? How do they sign it, where are they located, do they actually sign it or is it delegated to someone else, is it signed in the legal department or is it a smaller business with the CEO signing all contracts? At the end of the day, these simple questions can be highly elusive. It's very helpful to determine the signatory this early in the process and you'll gain more clarity about your prospect's authority level. If the individual you're working with says, "I sign," you can ask if they've made a purchase like this before. You can also ask if they made a purchase "this size" before to ensure they understand their own procurement process. As noted in Tip 35, there are many questions to ask about the procurement process; if you have difficulty determining some of the other important questions, at a minimum, find out who signs the contract.

Tip 40 Revalidate P2P with Your Sponsor

It's easy to lose your way as you progress on your path to purchase. Make sure all these key steps are incorporated into your 4-Phase Virtual Sales Process. Monitor your progress as you move into the presentation phase. You can revisit your P2P multiple times in a complex sale. Is there budget? Do you understand their procurement process? Do you know the participants who should attend your presentation? Do you know who will sign the order? Make sure you've covered the key elements of your qualification process as you move into your presentation and closing phases. Though there will be ample opportunity to further qualify in these phases, you're wasting valuable time if you're presenting to prospects who will be unable to purchase.

Chapter 3

Phase 3: Present

Chapter 3 reviews the virtual presentation and demonstration phase of our 4-Phase Virtual Sales Process. Virtual presentations are both an art and a science, and a fundamental building block of every virtual sales cycle. The virtual presentation is your time to shine - to impress the prospect with your depth of knowledge, your solution's efficacy, and how your solution will make an immediate impact. You should treat your presentation like a close - because it is. If you do a poor job of presenting, you will not get an opportunity to close.

Tip 41   Confirm Names, Titles, Roles of Attendees

In your Virtual Presentation, every detail counts. Make sure you know the key players who will attend your presentation. Use their names during the presentation, and understand the role each person plays in the decision-making process. Ultimately, you will need to convince the decision maker that your solution is the best fit to close the sale. If the decision maker will not be present, make sure you have identified your best path to ensure exposure and influence with this individual. Even if your internal sponsor is impressed, you can't close without the approval of the final decision maker.

Tip 42   Is There Anyone Else Who Should Attend?

Always ask your sponsor who else might be influential in the decision-making process and invite all of these key influencers to attend your presentation. This can eliminate multiple steps in the sales process and ensure you have not missed a crucial opinion in your process. For example, if you're selling a software solution which requires review by the IT Director, it's often better to have them involved early rather than finding this out later in the process. Key influencers can include business sponsors, administrators, end users, financial sponsors, and technical people. This varies significantly based upon your solution and sales process.

Tip 43   Virtual Presentation Alignment Call

Though every type of sale does not require a dedicated alignment call prior to the presentation, many do. Discuss the presentation with your sponsor and align the goals of your upcoming on-line meeting/presentation to ensure it will be effective for the target audience. Can you get your sponsor to verbally agree to move forward with an order if the presentation is a success? Has your sponsor laid out the process from this upcoming presentation through the final purchase? This call is a great opportunity to work with your internal sponsor to find out the remaining steps in the process and ascertain how much influence they might have in the final decision.

 **Power Tip**

There are many questions to ask (and for you to ponder) in a virtual presentation alignment call:

- What do they want shown in the presentation?

- Who are the decision makers?

- What do they consider most important to the decision makers (prioritize)?

- Who else should attend the presentation?

- What is the prospect's budget for this type of solution?

- What is the time frame to implement a solution?

- What other solutions, or vendors, are being considered?

- Do your services match well with the prospect's needs?

- Do we have enough agreement on the fundamentals to move forward in the process?

- Do they have the resources in place (or know where to find them) to make this project or purchase successful?

Tip 44   Revalidate the Reasons for Purchase

Make sure your internal sponsor (or the decision maker) completely understands the reasons why your solution is critical for their organization. Reiterate all the reasons they need to implement your solution and reassure them this is the only right decision. Always stay positive and reinforce the benefits of working with you. If there's pushback from certain key influencers, your validation process will help the internal sponsor respond appropriately and push forward toward a purchase. In other words, your internal sponsor should be able to clearly and succinctly reiterate your sales pitch, key benefits and value proposition.

Tip 45   Outline Your Online Presentation

Don't ever think about "winging it" for your virtual presentation. Plan ahead of time exactly what you want to say and how you want to say it. Anticipate objections and common questions, and have responses ready. Practice your presentation until you have many presentations under your belt and are completely comfortable with the material, path, technology, cadence and potential questions. Remember, you should always be the one controlling the flow of the meeting. Be prepared for anything from objections to technical issues and have a backup plan in place.

Tip 46   Incorporate the Virtual 'Good, Fast, Cheap Paradigm'

If you're leveraging the virtual model or at least some portion of this model such as a cost effective web sales model, it should be easy to show your prospects that your lower overhead allows you to focus on delivering high quality service, fast results and keen pricing. Instead of spending time on the road in planes, trains and automobiles, your virtual sales model allows you and your clients to enjoy the benefits of lower overhead and improved efficiency. This is contrary to the old cliché known as the 'Good, Fast, Cheap Paradigm'. In the old days, you could only pick two of these three attributes, today, using a virtual business (or sales model) your clients can realize all three, while you can still enjoy better margins. Remember to mention that your lower overhead and more efficient operation translate to a better value for your clients.

Tip 47 Create and Customize Your Virtual Presentation

Create a custom presentation for your prospects, don't use a cookie cutter presentation model. Each prospect is unique, and the solution you develop will vary for each of them. Demonstrate how your model incorporates custom fit solutions for the specific needs of each partner. Listen to the prospects' needs, and be flexible enough to adapt your services and delivery to fit those needs. This is as valid for landscape services and surround-sound systems as it is for software solutions.

 **Power Tip**

Avoid focusing on what you want to show your prospect, and instead focus on what they came to see and hear. Ask about their goals for the Web meeting and carefully listen to their response. Don't assume you know their goals, even if you had an alignment call. Let your prospect tell you what they want and need, and then explain how your solution fits those needs. This technique will help you properly guide the flow of the presentation while improving the likelihood of a successful outcome.

Tip 48 Review and Rehearse the Presentation

Practice your presentation with a friend or colleague or review it with your team. Virtual presentations must be carefully rehearsed and delivered in a timely manner. Many experienced web presentation experts agree that a one hour presentation is often the maximum amount of time salespeople should consider for their presentations. You want a concise, compelling and problem free presentation. Regardless of how many presentations you've done, mistakes can happen if you are poorly prepared, and even minor mistakes can derail your sales process. Have a colleague play the part of a difficult prospect. Role play can dramatically improve your presentation technique, timing and delivery. Your colleagues should ask tough questions and raise challenging objections. The more prepared you are, the greater the likelihood of a successful outcome.

Power Tip

Rehearse, prepare, plan — but don't read from a script. The best virtual presentations sound natural, as if you're speaking to a business associate, friend or neighbor. The primary reason for planning, practicing and preparing is to give you the knowledge and confidence to counter any argument, and overcome any objection during the presentation. This means being flexible, adaptable, and spontaneous. Think of your presentation outline and rehearsal as a guideline to follow, but not a script to recite from memory. Reading from a canned script typically results in a boring presentation.

In-Depth Review

If you're using more than one web presenter, and the second presenter is in a remote location, practice the screen presentation hand-off between your PC and theirs. Rehearse this hand-off multiple times to ensure a smooth transition. If you're selected to "push" the slides or screens for the second speaker, thus eliminating presentation transfers, make sure you carefully rehearse your interactions to ensure a professional result for your audience. This may sound simple, but it can be tricky even for web presentation veterans. The interplay between multiple speakers may not come naturally, that's why you should jointly practice the presentation to get a sense of your partner's speaking style, verbal cues, preferences and cadence. The most effective and natural multi-speaker presentations are the result of practice and familiarity. There are major differences between an interactive web meeting presentation and a one-to-many webinar presentation. We've encountered speakers who are very comfortable with interactive sessions, yet require much more training and preparation for a larger scale, non-interactive webinar presentations.

Tip 49 Create a List of Questions You Want to Ask

As with every aspect of your virtual presentation, you want to be thoroughly prepared. Part of this preparation includes asking questions of your audience. This interaction allows them to participate in the meeting, to raise objections that you can and will address, and to help you build credibility and rapport with your prospects. Your questions will help prime the pump, resulting in a truly interactive session with your prospects. This makes for a much more effective virtual presentation.

Tip 50 Make Sure You Address Audience Specific Issues

During your presentation, ask your prospects to verbalize their needs, wants and concerns. Respond to each point they make by explaining exactly how your solution will address that specific item. Your prospects may not know precisely what they need or want, so be ready to ask questions to facilitate an interactive dialogue. Close the loop at the end of the presentation by inquiring if each of these key issues/challenges has been addressed.

Tip 51 Make Your Content Concise and Compelling

Make your presentation dynamic. Use instant polling, graphics, and live solution and website examples whenever possible. Leverage website video and social media examples, client testimonials (and/or video testimonials), and other Web marketing materials. Always show rather than tell. Go live to websites instead of just talking about them. Show software solutions live, don't use PowerPoint screens or flat images, do a live Google search to demonstrate SEO results, show a client testimonial by navigating to your website. These techniques will engage your audience, they are far more compelling than simply talking about what you do and referring to a PowerPoint slide.

 **Real-World Scenario**

When presenting financial information or Excel spreadsheets, make sure the number in the bottom right corner tells a story. Business people are trained to look at the top row, left-hand column and then the bottom right corner to quickly glean the gist of any type of spreadsheet. Not long ago, a client of mine showed me a PowerPoint slide he intended to use in a webinar presentation, the title was "Fuel Price Savings." The left-hand column showed four weeks in the month of June, the next several columns included breakout data, and the column on the far right was weekly savings. The bottom right-hand corner showed savings for the month, an amount of $710. The number was not boldfaced, highlighted, or expanded upon in any way. It was also a very small number. "What are you trying to say here?" I asked. The presenter said his program could save trucking companies over $700 per month if they used their unique fuel procurement approach. "That's too small a number," I said. "Nobody will care." But, if you took that number ($710) and multiplied it by 12 months ($8,520) and applied it to a trucking company that operated a fleet of 125 trucks, the savings would be over $1 million per year. Because the webinar targeted large trucking companies and not owner operators (individual truck drivers), fleet executives would definitely notice that number. Furthermore, the presenter said that 90 percent of all clients saved a significant amount on their ongoing fuel purchases. Now we had a compelling story for the presentation. The calculation at the bottom of the spreadsheet was shown in very large, boldfaced numbers. We added an arrow pointing to it from the bottom right-hand corner. We changed the slide's title to "Over $1 Million in Fuel Savings for 125 Trucks." The presentation was very compelling with these changes, conveying an important story, with this slide as the focal point.

Tip 52   Be a Web Presentation Expert

No one wants to buy from an amateur, from someone who is fumbling through a presentation, unprepared to take advantage of the time and opportunity offered. You must instill confidence that you (and your business) are the best possible choice for this prospect. Know your own value proposition inside and out, and make sure you clearly and succinctly explain the benefits, improvements and ROI your solution offers. Proficiency with your web presentation system is essential and will help you look and sound highly credible. This means you can easily navigate through animations and annotations, change screens and speakers and do so while promoting, dismissing and recording. Be an expert at both your web meeting software and your Web presentation methodology. It is truly surprising how often this step is overlooked.

Tip 53   Customize Your Presentation

Customize each presentation and demo, assuming you're selling considered purchase solutions (where the price point justifies the time investment). Use your prospect's logo, website images and information, annual report data, or a photo of your prospects' home or garden (or a similar home) if you're selling B2C solutions. Tailor the presentation specifically to your audience, including industry and titles. This method is effective for virtually any business, including software solutions, financial planners, realtors, kitchen designers, marketing agencies or landscape companies. Regardless of the solution you sell, strive to make the presentation specifically relevant to your audience.

 **Real-World Scenario**

"The other company seemed to better understand the specifics of our business," said a prospect. This is not something you want to hear. Your prospects might feel this way because you're using general presentation materials, language and terms. Customize your materials for both the industry and the specific prospect or organization. If you are selling to architects, your presentation should utilize jargon specific to their industry. Photos and images should be germane to architects. Your entire presentation should convey your knowledge, understanding and experience with their type of needs. One of the vertical markets StartUpSelling, Inc. targets is the insurance agency market. For this vertical we would use jargon like: book of business, producer, hard market (or soft market), personal lines, commercial insurance, benefits, group plans, work comp, experience mods, X-date, etc. Our understanding of the industry specifics and the methods used to convey our expertise in our presentations helps us demonstrate our proficiency with this vertical market and the target audience. Prior to our presentation, we review every prospect's website to ensure our presentations focus specifically on their agency business and target markets. StartMarketingTech targets B2B organizations including technology and software companies. Our value proposition and jargon target these types of organizations as opposed to insurance agencies. Make sure your presentation demonstrates your vertical expertise and knowledge of your designated target market.

Tip 54   Agenda, Introductions, Follow-Up Plans, Goals

An important aspect of any sales presentation is controlling the flow of the meeting. Creating an agenda and displaying it at the beginning of your Web meeting can help you keep your meeting on track. The agenda should provide clear and simple guidance for the meeting, covering the key topics and order of your presentation. While the exact delivery can change, at a minimum, the audience will understand the general meeting objectives and content. Introductions are also important, both for you and your prospects. Beyond the agenda, you will have additional goals you seek to accomplish. Rapport and relationship building will be important to your follow-up plans. Next steps should be determined prior, during and upon completion of the meeting — see Tip #56 for more on this.

Tip 55   Determine the ROI for This Sale and How To Present It

ROI is one of the key factors required when closing many types of sales. As detailed in Tip 32, you have probably taken the time to research the ROI and have specific calculations and a detailed explanation of both your hard and soft ROI. Ensure that this information is presented during your Web meeting and be prepared to offer compelling and concise answers for your attendees. Remember, if you can show them the calculations, it's often better than merely discussing them.

Tip 56   Agree on the Next Steps in Advance

Maintain control over your presentation by anticipating what will happen next. Don't adhere to a strict script, but strive to achieve your pre-designated goals with your presentation. Knowing the next steps in the sales process is a critical goal. Establish next steps with your sponsor in advance of the Web meeting and make sure they help you understand the political landscape of the meeting, who is the decision maker, and which key influencers can make or break your sale. If the next steps will be based on the success of this meeting and cannot be determined in advance, attempt to validate these steps as your meeting comes to a close. If next steps cannot be determined, make sure you've scheduled a summary meeting with your sponsor to help you move forward in your Path to Purchase. Always keep moving the sales cycle forward. Qualify, simplify and consistently work on your P2P.

 **Power Tip**

Use a before and after approach for your presentations whenever possible. For example, show the current annual expenditures before your solution is implemented, and the reduced expenditure after completion. Show current labor expenditures and the improved productivity and decreased labor costs after implementation of your solution. Show lower customer satisfaction ratings at a similar company before they added your unique innovations, and dramatically improved customer service experience after their rollout. If you're selling home renovations to upscale homeowners, use before and after photographs, preferably of similar homes. You might offer a quick mock-up of what the actual prospect home will look like. Your presentation might be the result of 5, 10 or 20 hours of identification and qualification efforts, so make it a highly engaging and professional experience, and when possible, leverage specific before and after examples.

Tip 57   Beware of the Boring PowerPoint

Even after you've customized your presentation, if it uses predominately textual PowerPoint slides, the presentation tends to be boring. As mentioned in prior tips, show action on your screen, live solutions, live websites, software demonstrations, before and after examples, images, stories, etc. On average, PowerPoint slides take one minute per slide to review. Of course this varies dramatically by speaker and topic and web meeting versus webinar. Use your PowerPoint slide show as the framework to demonstrate your solution's efficacy. Keep your audience engaged with entertaining stories related to your business, live demonstrations of your solution or service in action, and comparisons between the prospect's current circumstances and your solution (before and after). A bored prospect is unlikely to listen to you long enough to buy, and even if they do listen long enough, the mediocre presentation will likely produce a poor result.

 **Power Tip**

PowerPoint animation and screen transitions, such as making lines display one at a time or using special effects to move from screen to screen, should be used sparingly in virtual presentations. These special functions can slow you down and be confusing sometimes due to the variable time lag between your screen and your verbal presentation. Effective PowerPoint presentations should incorporate images, white space and a limited number of bullets on each slide. Opinions on this vary widely, but many agree that a five bullet maximum is a reasonable starting point. Always avoid verbose slides. Instead, make your slides readable and engaging. Make sure your branding is professional. A modest logo on the bottom right corner of each screen, and your company's color as an accent throughout the PowerPoint will help convey your branding professionally. However, the branding should be subtle and secondary to the important solution content you wish to convey.

Tip 58   Test the Technology in Advance!

In advance of your major presentation, test the actual PC that will be used in the conference room or office and test the projector, too. If you're using a collaborative meeting solution, such as GoToMeeting, perform a test run ahead of time. Make sure any remote presentation speakers or participants test their PCs and speakerphone equipment, Internet connectivity, and knowledge of the software. If at all possible, have a back up ready in the event of a failure. Ask yourself, "What is the worst that could happen?" and be prepared for that scenario. Find out before the presentation if a critical piece of equipment or software isn't working properly, if the prospect's firewall is preventing you from using their conference room PC, or if you might encounter some other technical or logistics issue.

In-Depth Review

The Actual Presentation: 10 Helpful Hints to Ensure a Great Virtual Presentation

1. Start your virtual meeting early. Try starting 15-20 minutes before a major Web seminar, and 10 minutes before a small virtual group presentation.

2. Assuming this is a web meeting (as opposed to a webinar), as soon as you begin ask your audience if they can hear you clearly and see your screen correctly.

3. Explain how the technology (GoToMeeting, GoToWebinar, WebEx, Adobe, LiveMeeting, etc.) works.

4. Have your presentation material open and ready to go. All other software (Outlook, Skype, etc.) that is not going to be part of the presentation should be closed.

5. Eliminate disturbing background noises. Make sure windows are closed to reduce street noise. Put mobile devices and cell phones on silent mode. Close your office door. Set your desk phone to voice-mail. If there are other people in the area, make sure they know you are doing an important presentation and cannot be disturbed. You can even tape a sign to your office door stating that you're in a presentation and cannot be disturbed. More than one embarrassing moment has been avoided using this low tech technique.

6. Ask your audience how much time they have for the presentation. This makes you look professional, lets you determine how much material you'll be able to review, and will make your prospect feel you truly value their time.

7. Introduce yourself and anyone else from your team involved in the presentation. Make sure everyone at the presentation knows who everyone else is.

8. Review your agenda. This helps set audience expectations for the presentation, as well as time frames.

9. Keep in mind that your audience may use a speakerphone. Speak clearly and distinctly, and be prepared to repeat yourself when necessary. Ask questions during the presentation to ensure the attendees can hear you and are following the presentation.

10. At the end of the presentation, reiterate your key points, establish firm next steps, and thank your prospects for their time.

Tip 59 Create a Vision of Your Ultimate Destination

Decide what your desired outcome is for the presentation. In some cases, it may be a signature. In others, your desired outcome may be a follow-up presentation with the decision maker, or a request to submit a proposal. It is critical, however, to envision where you ultimately see your presentation leading. As the saying goes, if you don't know where you want to go, you'll never get there.

Tip 60 Evaluate the Political Landscape *After* the Presentation

Immediately following your presentation, collaborate with your team and discuss the results. Get both strategic and tactical feedback. Strategically, their feedback will help you become a better presenter in the future. Tactically, a colleague may have picked up on something said (or unsaid) during the presentation that offers important insight into the thought process of your prospect. Discuss the tenor of the meeting following your presentation — did the prospect seem enthusiastic? Was the decision maker impressed? Evaluate questions and comments made by the prospect that could indicate their level of interest, such as "If we want to implement this, how soon would we need to start?" Or, "How much lead time do we need to get into your delivery queue?" Or, "If we take this proposal to the CFO, are all costs clearly noted?" A strategic and tactical review of each presentation provides an excellent opportunity to better assess your likelihood of closing the sale.

Tip 61 Determine If Additional Buy-In Is Required

For complex sales, there will be times you will meet someone new who may be critical to the buying process. If there are multiple owners, a committee, partners or a board of directors who must approve your deal, get this information as early on as possible, and tailor your presentation to this new individual or group. Don't assume you know all the key players in your potential deal, and make sure you have an opportunity to virtually meet or influence all of them.

Tip 62 Revisit Your Prospect Scorecard

Using your Prospect Scorecard is essential during the sales process. It is not enough to say that a prospect looks promising, or is exhibiting "buying behaviors." At StartUpSelling, Inc. we use a relatively simple, but powerful qualifier called "BUD," or budget, urgency, decision maker. We then rate our prospects on a 1-to-5 scale for key buying attributes (e.g., company size, outsourcing orientation, etc.). When we are speaking with decision makers, and the prospect scores higher than "3," they're very likely to buy if there is a budget and any type of urgency. For example, if the prospect is rated a "3," and they need to increase the number of prospects in their pipeline and have a marketing budget for this initiative, we are very likely to add a new client. There are many other qualifying acronyms you can use, such as BUNT (budget, urgency, need, timing). Regardless of the acronym you select for your sales cycle, make sure you strictly adhere to it and modify the Scorecard ranking after each sales presentation.

Tip 63   Architecture, Environment and Technical Details

It is important to know your audience and the purpose of your presentation before you embark upon your presentation. If the decision maker approved the purchase of your solution, and handed you off to the technical team, limit the business discussions, and solution benefits and focus on the technical details. Likewise, if you're meeting with the decision makers, don't bog them down with the technical minutia of your solution. Plan the right presentation for your audience and purpose.

Tip 64   Back-Up Plans Help Ensure Success

According to Murphy's Law, anything that can go wrong will go wrong. Prepare ahead of time for any issues that may arise. Send a copy of your final PowerPoint presentation to a colleague, and practice it with them beforehand. That way, if you experience a power outage, an Internet disruption, your telephone disconnects, or other unforeseen problem, your colleague can seamlessly continue the presentation. You can also send your presentation directly to your prospect ensuring you have a back-up plan in the event of an Internet failure. If they have your PowerPoint and a phone line available, your presentation can continue. Don't assume these failures can't happen — on occasion they can, and will. Of the thousands of online presentations we've done, there have been times when we needed to use our back-up systems, and thankfully, we had them in place and were able to continue successfully. Have a back-up plan (or two) in place. You will rarely need it, but when you do, it may save your deal.

 **Real-World Scenario**

Several years ago, I presented virtually to a group of approximately 50 attendees. They were in a classroom setting 1,000 miles away, as I presented a sophisticated, cloud-based client survey solution. They had speakers attached to a PC and a large projection screen at the front of the classroom. The audience included account managers responsible for customer satisfaction, and they wanted to ensure this solution would be acceptable to their clients. The investment for this system could exceed six figures, therefore, this presentation needed to go smoothly. Although senior management had already confirmed their desire to purchase, this validation presentation could make, or break, the sale.

Prior to the meeting, we tested all of the equipment we intended to use to make sure everything was compatible and worked perfectly. We tested the speakers to ensure attendees could hear us at the back of the room. The internal sponsor reviewed the agenda and offered suggestions about specific features we needed to show. We added a question-and-answer session to the end of the presentation, and our sponsor provided us with the types of questions he expected. The internal sponsor polled the audience for questions and wrote them on a white board while he simultaneously read them to me so I could hear the questions clearly. The actual presentation went flawlessly, the attendees were very impressed, and the Q&A session was very professional and interactive. The sale was completed, which was not a surprising result considering the advanced planning and preparation for this virtual presentation. When you have a large opportunity, plan, prepare and capitalize on it!

Tip 65 Use Both VOIP and Telephony For Online Presentations

Use a high quality USB headset for any online presentation, Skype call, or other Internet-based communication. A USB headset (as of this writing) typically delivers the best quality audio, and leaves your hands free to use the mouse or keyboard. We also recommend choosing cloud based software that offers both VoIP and telephony-based audio. There are several reasons for these recommendations. First, not everyone in your audience may have a USB headset or quality built-in speakers for audio. Second, VoIP uses up bandwidth, and may cause lag issues for presenters or attendees with slower Internet connections. Finally, having both VoIP and telephony available provides the presenter a back-up option if one or the other is interrupted.

Tip 66   Invest In High-Speed Internet

Online presentations may require a relatively large amount of bandwidth and DSL speeds or slower cable speeds may not suffice. Cable providers offer business-class service for around $99 per month and many guarantee same day service in the event of an outage. Fast Internet connectivity is the foundation for any web sales operation or cloud computing-based virtual company. Invest in the highest quality Internet connectivity your budget will allow. Use a high quality router (these are very inexpensive) to deliver and receive the signal at speeds required for your presentation. When possible hardwire your laptop or PC to the router, and at a minimum, do so during your online presentations. Hardwired connections are always best, less prone to interference and offer better throughput than wireless connectivity.

Tip 67   Client Quotes, Name Dropping and References

Name dropping can be a great sales tool, important in traditional presentations and more so for web presentations. Drop the name of one or more clients who are well known or respected in your prospect's industry. If your prospect hears that one of their industry leaders has signed with you, it often can be the deciding factor in closing the sale. If a prospect asks for references, you should be prepared to provide these, but use them as a closing tool. For example, ask for assurance that your prospect will purchase, assuming your references are top notch. Your references are extremely valuable, and should be treated as an important asset. Don't burn your clients' time with repeated reference requests unless you're confident a reference check will lead to a close. When possible, leverage pithy client quotes and compelling case studies to mitigate the need for actual reference calls.

⚠ Watch-Out Tip

Take the high road when it comes to competitors. I remember a sales executive who came from a competitor. He was very happy to have landed at our company, and somewhat disgruntled about his prior employer. During a conference call, the sales executive made a negative statement about a competitor, his former employer. It is unprofessional to do so, and I called the prospective client afterwards to apologize. The prospect said they appreciated the call very much and were somewhat "taken aback" by the negative comments. Ultimately, they signed with our company and we were fortunate our sale was not compromised by the negativity. Focus on your strengths, and never bad mouth a competitor. Here's one way to couch your words, "Our solution is implemented much faster than other solutions, you will be up and running two weeks earlier with our unique methodology as opposed to other companies in our industry." This type of statement focuses on your strengths, stating you are better than other competitors, without singling out a competitor and making negative statements about them. Remember to back up your statements by offering client testimonials, case studies and ROI calculations.

Tip 68   Prepare for Questions about Pricing or Discounts

You should have standard pricing in place, but occasionally you may need to negotiate with the prospect in order to secure the deal. Be prepared for this ahead of time. Know all aspects of your profit margins, and determine what you must have in order to make the sale worthwhile. Avoid discount strategies in favor of reducing premium services to lower the investment requirements. That said, you must still deliver a quality solution, so you can't remove critical services if they are necessary for successful delivery. For example, if you're an arborist, you can still provide high quality pruning, but cut costs by leaving the branches on site. If you offer client satisfaction surveys, suggest the client surveys the top third of their clients instead of the top 50%. Determine if budget is the issue or value is the issue. If it is the latter, your prospect has not fully bought into your value proposition and your prospect may need to be reminded about what makes you better and worth the investment quoted. When necessary, you can also offer volume discounts, a discount for a longer duration contract, or a bundled services discount. At the end of the day, you need to protect your profit margin to ensure you deliver a quality solution.

Tip 69   Follow Up: Send a Personal Email, Make a Phone Call

Show your prospect you value their business by sending a personalized follow-up email. The email also lets them know they can expect to receive this type of attention once they become a client. If possible, send a personalized email and place a call to each attendee to thank them for their time. Ask them if they care to offer feedback, and if some of the feedback is negative, don't become defensive. Thank them for their candor, as this might be some of the most valuable advice you will ever receive. Incorporate all feedback into future presentations.

Tip 70   Check for Buying Signals (Buying Signs)

Were there buying signals during the meeting? Perhaps a few forward looking questions were asked, or positive comments were made about your solution. During your web meetings, listen for positive feedback, enthusiasm about your solution, questions referring to probable start dates, or the decision maker naming someone on their side as the project lead. These behaviors signal an improving likelihood of purchase and should be capitalized on quickly. Be prepared to send out your proposal (order confirmation) immediately. Establish an agreement in principle verbally or through an email commitment. Though these aren't binding, they are an important psychological building block in your Path to Purchase (P2P). At a minimum, establish firm next steps toward closure as you move into your Virtual Closing Phase.

CHAPTER 4

Phase 4: Close

Chapter 4 reviews the final phase of the 4-Phase Virtual Sales Process, the commitment and closure phase. There are many theories about closing, from the ABCs of closing (e.g., Always Be Closing) to the never-need-to-close approach (closing is a gradual process and if done right, you never need to ask for the order). My closing methodology is both an art and a science, though I leverage a web centric and empirical process. Closing the virtual sale should be exciting, rewarding, profitable and fun. This chapter will help you learn how to ensure a successful web based closing methodology. Chapter 4 also includes the final tip, the essence of a web sales and virtual business operation — the benefits of the virtual lifestyle. Surely, all of our challenges cannot be solved by going virtual, but I'm confident it is an important step in the right direction from both a business and lifestyle perspective. Moving from a traditional sales process to a web based sales process will dramatically improve any small business, emerging business or even corporate sales force working within the confines of yesterday's traditional brick-and-mortar model.

Tip 71   Trial Close: Ask for the Order

When should you ask for the order? As you progress deeper into the process, try a trial close. This means simply asking for the order or the likelihood of the order which can be done in a web meeting, conference call or even an email. For example, "You've been reviewing our solution for several weeks now and both you and your team were very impressed by our presentation. What needs to be done to finalize an agreement?" Don't be afraid to trial close, if you've followed your P2P, it's unlikely that your internal sponsor would be offended in any way. Further, any objections offer clear opportunities to determine what work still needs to be done. If you already have the commitment, determine and validate the steps necessary to finalize the order and receive a signature or purchase order. Ask for the business, and then ask for the completion of each of the steps required to obtain closure.

 **Power Tip**

Trial closing should be one of the easiest aspects of the virtual closing process, particularly if you use hypothetical questions or forward looking statements when phrasing your trial closing questions and suggestions. For example, our team recently presented a marketing and lead generation program to a prospect that was in-profile and qualified. The presentation went well, and the prospect responded very positively. This created a perfect opportunity for a trial close. I began by saying, "It sounds to me like we have a great fit, and that our programs would address your needs." They agreed. I continued and asked, "What would we need to do to make your team comfortable enough to begin a project?" After a long pause, they asked if we could provide some type of solution at a price point that would better fit their budget. They had already decided they would like to work with us, but we simply exceeded their current budget allocation. A casual trial close uncovered their final objection, and they signed an amended proposal a few days later. We offered a revised solution, extending their contract term and lowering the monthly fee, in essence allowing them to "lease" our products and services. They quickly agreed to the terms and signed our simple Order Confirmation.

Tip 72 Would You Buy It If It Cost a Dollar?

A great technique to help identify and overcome objections is to ask a leading trial close question, "If this solution was only a dollar, would you purchase it?" These types of questions remove the pricing and investment objections and determine if the prospect really wants your solution. If they will buy it for a dollar, euro or peso, you can then work with the prospect to determine a path where they could and would purchase your solution. You may still need to overcome value objections, investment thresholds or political challenges, but at least you know they want your solution.

Tip 73 Validate the Decision If You Get the 'Green Light' on the Purchase

Once you are given the go ahead, emphatically state that you are very happy to be working with your new client and they have made a great decision moving forward with your solution and company. Succinctly reiterate how this purchase will benefit them, and thank them not only for their business but also for their assistance in working with you throughout the sales process. Proper validation helps eliminate the possibility of your prospect reneging on a commitment (buyer's remorse), and validation helps start the relationship off in a positive manner.

Tip 74 Negotiations Can Occur Before, During, and After the Close

Even if you have an agreement in principal with your sponsor, who might be the owner, president, CEO or sole authority of a household, you may still need to finalize details with a purchasing department, finance person, legal department (see Tip 75) or for consumers, a bank or leasing entity. Items such as pricing, terms and legal jargon will have differing levels of importance to each party involved with the purchase. Be prepared to adjust language or terms where possible, but do not make concessions or revisions that will negatively impact your profit margins or nullify your pricing structure. Separate your business terms, which should already have been agreed upon, from legal terms and requirements. For example, it's reasonable for the purchasing department to better define a net 30 terms clause, but they should not be allowed to mandate a 5% discount for standard payment terms. Also, beware of procurement departments insisting on extended terms like 60 day payment terms because they are "required." If they threaten to slow down your deal, seek the assistance of your sponsor.

Tip 75 Legal Departments Can Impede Your Deal

This tip is not meant in a disparaging way. Lawyers and contract departments are supposed to haggle over contractual details, and many are measured by the types of changes they negotiate. In some cases attorneys are on the clock and clients might expect them to show the resulting contractual improvements to prove the value of their services. Their job is to protect their client, which may run contrary to reasonable and fair best practices for your sales agreement or business. You need to separate legal issues from business issues. For example, if an attorney tells you that the company will only accept Net 60 terms for payment, as opposed to your Net 10, and your sponsor has agreed to the Net 10 terms, argue that this is a business term, not a legal term (if you want to show flexibility on this particular point, compromise at Net 30, don't agree to Net 60 terms). If the attorney says you must include a termination-at-will clause, when your contract is in effect for six months, this is a change to the business terms and should not be allowed. To counter this, tell the attorney that their clause "changes the business terms of the agreement by making it a one-month agreement and the pricing will be dramatically higher if it is a one month agreement." Or you can say that you don't accept clients on a month-to-month agreement. Remember, in most cases, the attorneys or contract specialists simply want to improve the contract to benefit their company or client. If you cannot accommodate their requests, go back to your sponsor and clearly explain the road block, they will typically intervene on your behalf. When doing this, however, make sure you know all of the issues which are "deal breakers" as you only want to reach out to your sponsor once. If necessary, and if allowed, arrange a joint meeting (con call or web meeting) with your sponsor and their legal department to cut through any red tape.

 **Power Tip**

When working with a legal department or contract department, determine which issues are minor and which are major, and work to keep your legal fees and time investment as low as possible. For example, if you sell technology and there is an intellectual property (IP) issue this will likely be a major item, one which you may not be able to negotiate. Your company may deem that you own the technology, it is your intellectual property and it cannot be "owned" by your prospective client, whereas the determination of specific arbitration rules may be less difficult to resolve and not considered a major roadblock. Be certain you determine if there are two separate contractual processes — legal and purchasing. If this is the case, it's even more important to separate business issues from legal issues. For example, let's say the legal department is discussing payment terms. Your response should be, "That item has already been discussed and negotiated." If the business sponsor wants extended payment terms you can say that, "there needs to be a corresponding increase in their purchase price." Or, you can respond by explaining it is a business issue, not a legal issue. This won't work all the time, but it works often and can help set the tone for business vs. legal parameters in your discussions. For small business sales, or B2C sales, you can often use a short order form or boilerplate contract (we often refer to this as an Order Confirmation) to bypass legal scrutiny, resulting in rapid execution. This can even be done with larger sales and has worked very well for many years, across many types of businesses. Simplify your legal documents and streamline these processes whenever possible. It's always best to consult with your own attorney, but remember it's usually better to limit the time spent on contracts and increase the time spent servicing clients. Great service often mitigates litigious issues.

Tip 76 Reference the Delivery Date with the Reverse Timeline

Consistently instill urgency into the process by referring to the completion, rollout or delivery date. This is one of the many benefits of creating a Reverse Timeline, as outlined in Tip 31. If your prospect requires a solution which must be delivered in 90 days, and you have illustrated an effective program will require 75 days for production and delivery, you can push for a signature within two weeks, without sounding "pushy." The Reverse Timeline provides both parties with a framework to track and monitor contract execution and delivery goals, and often eliminates the possibility of additional competition, as a prospect realizes they do not have time to secure additional proposals without impacting their delivery date. Leverage the Reverse Timeline as a catalyst for closure.

Tip 77 Track Weekly Sales Activity – It's Your Business Barometer

An agile virtual salesperson or business must monitor sales activity to determine if and when a change of direction, reallocation of resources or an adjustment of focus needs to be made. Web based selling provides a competitive advantage over traditional selling models, and is best leveraged with continual adjustments and refinements. Create a simple mechanism for tracking sales activity. Rolling reports on basic spreadsheets are often fast, simple and efficient and can be used by most salespeople and businesses regardless of size. Contact management and sales force automation systems can also be used, just be wary of the time you're investing in the actual maintenance and upkeep of your tracking systems. For example, monitor your outbound calling and its effectiveness. If you're better on the phone in the morning, then you should make immediate adjustments to increase your morning calls and to focus on other activities in the afternoon. This can be tracked easily by listing total appointments booked by week, while alternating between morning and afternoon calling. Within a month, you will have sufficient data to make refinements as needed. See the next In-Depth Review for a sample rolling report.

Tip 78 Keep a Balance Between 'Doing' and 'Tracking'

Nimble web salespeople and virtual businesses should spend most of their time doing, and a modest amount of time tracking. Begin by determining what key factors need to be measured for you to succeed (some businesses refer to these as KPI's or Key Performance Indicators). These typically can be narrowed to a few key metrics or ratios, such as:

- Cold calls per appointment.

- Appointments per closed sale.

- Proposals per closed sale.

- Profit margin per sale.

- Gross profit per customer or contract.

After developing an effective system for monitoring your sales activity and ratios, tracking should be limited to no more that 5 percent of your daily sales time. At StartUpSelling, Inc., this task is accomplished by measuring outbound call efficiency, appointment activity and results, and a prospect pipeline. Each is monitored in a simple rolling report on one tab of an Excel workbook, making navigation simple and updates fast. The rolling report concept is extremely helpful to many salespeople, providing easy ongoing analysis with nominal effort. Allow the report to roll down the spreadsheet forever, totaling results at the bottom. These can then be sliced and diced by week, month, year, product, etc. The key is successful tracking without allowing paralysis by analysis.

 **In-Depth Review**

We think closing is both an art and a science, incorporating subtleties such as personality dynamics, competing project and budget initiatives, timing and company (or family) politics. That's why you need an objective methodology to monitor and track closing, and your Prospect Scorecard qualifying acronym, to help quantify your closing opportunities. Utilizing your qualifying acronym, BUD for example, and creating a simple spreadsheet to track the source of prospects which ultimately close, will improve your long term close ratio.

The image below shows a sample sales tracking spreadsheet. For example, let's say we scheduled 10 prospect demonstrations (or meetings) in May, and nine actually transpired. Six of these resulted in a proposal and three purchased. The buyers came from an e-marketing campaign, LinkedIn inquiry and a client referral. The ratios of appointments, proposals per appointment, closes per appointment and closes per proposal all update automatically. This ultra-simple chart allows a virtual salesperson to quickly and easily monitor their closing ratio, and determine which activities are working and what needs to be modified.

Date	Demo?	Proposal?	Closed?	Source
9/1	1	1	1	Emarketing
9/4	1	1	0	LinkedIn
9/7	1	0	0	Web Seminar (May)
9/12	1	1	0	Emarketing
9/14	1	0	0	Google Search - SEO
9/17	1	1	1	Emarketing
9/20	0	0	0	Article Directory
9/22	1	1	0	Blog
9/24	1	1	1	Web Seminar (July)
9/28	1	0	0	Emarketing
10	**9**	**6**	**3**	
Close Ratio % Prospects		67%	33%	*Goal: Close 25% of Appointments*
Close Ratio % Proposals			50%	*Goal: Close 40% of Proposals*

Tip 79 Closing Using a Requirements Assessment Analysis

A requirements assessment analysis is a great closing technique for many types of sales, from swimming pool installations, to project-related or complex sales. It is often critical for large-scale implementations and rollouts. If you do not fully analyze the needs and the scope of the necessary work, how will you effectively design your solution? How will you properly structure pricing? How will you satisfy your customer? Use a requirements assessment analysis to help define the scope of a project, gain trust and knowledge and win the deal. Requirements assessment analysis can include project milestones, implementation schedules, schedules for roll out timelines, team interviews, end user interviews, training, budget allocation, solution and service selection and ROI, to mention just a few key areas that might be reviewed. The story in the Power Tip below illustrates how a requirements assessment analysis can not only be important to creating the most accurate proposal, but also can be a powerful closing tool.

 **Power Tip**

After presenting the reverse timeline, I could see that both our internal sponsor and the decision maker were impressed with our custom training solution. Mr. Jones, the decision maker, expressed concern about being behind schedule and needing to make a decision very quickly, but was not sufficiently comfortable to move forward with a large scale order. This was an opportune time to propose a Training Requirements Assessment Analysis (TRA), something I created specifically for these types of situations. After explaining how the analysis would help them, and that they would receive a full credit for the expenditure if they moved forward with us, we discussed the nuances of this important step in their process. The assessment analysis would result in our expert consultants meeting with key members of their project team, key managers from each region, and selected end users to become familiar with their needs, training requirements and specific goals and challenges. After these interviews, and a comprehensive review of the software platform they intended to implement, our consultants could then determine how many users needed training, how many languages would be required, required venues for training, the types of training deliverables required including classroom, web based training, on demand training, train the trainer, etc. This would be highly advantageous for Mr. Jones, as it would provide a detailed plan explaining exactly what needed to be done, for whom it would be done, when it needed to be accomplished and how much time and money it would take to complete. He would be given a clear, specific and actionable rollout plan. It was also advantageous for our sales process, as we gained intimate knowledge of the pending project, and we could built rapport with members of the team who would be involved with the project. Though their investment in the assessment analysis could be credited toward their project deliverables, if they chose someone else, the TRA represented work which needed to be accomplished and it would save them time and money relating to the costs associated with another vendor. Mr. Jones quickly signed a contract for Training Requirements Assessment Analysis and about six weeks later, he signed a major agreement for a custom training rollout.

Tip 80 Close with Interesting and Compelling Stories

Short, relevant and emotional stories are a powerful method to convince prospects that they should select your solution. Stories allow your prospect to better relate to you, your solution and your company (a good source on using stories to convey a message can be found in *Made To Stick* by the Heath brothers). Stories tend to sound less like a sales pitch and more like someone trying to communicate. Sharing a story helps convey empathy and is a highly effective method for building rapport. Prospects are often more willing to listen to a story than a continuing diatribe of features, functions and benefits. Think of these stories as you might think back to a childhood fable. There was a basic plot line with a clear result that delivered a simple but important message, such as *The Tortoise and the Hare* and *The Boy Who Cried Wolf* from Aesop or the more current *The Gift of The Magi* by O. Henry. Short, interesting, emotional and relevant stories will enhance your value proposition and increase the probability a prospect will buy. Try to think of short stories that highlight your dedication to customers, your rapid response, creative solutions or remarkable success rate. Give specific examples of your achievements in a story format, with client names, locations, challenges and results.

 **Real-World Scenario**

"Not long ago, I sold a million dollar deal by telling a simple, two minute story. Perhaps this seems hard to believe, but let me retell the story and you can decide." Note how the first sentence of this "story" represents an interesting beginning, designed to grab the attention of the audience by making a bold claim and promising a few relevant details to validate that claim. Here is the essence of the story, it was successful for me, and a similar version can be successful for you.

Early in my career, I worked as the director of sales for a computer reseller that targeted large corporations. It was a fiercely competitive market, selling commoditized products, and margins were usually slim. One day, we were speaking with the decision maker and two key influencers of a very large company, a great account opportunity for a company our size. We needed something to convince them to move forward with us, as opposed to the many other vendors they could select. Stating we offered great pricing and service would simply be echoing the same thing every vendor said. So, I asked them if I could share a brief story that would explain why they should select us as their vendor. Here's a paraphrase of what I said, the story of *The Old Wooden Desk*.

"*I work in an old building, circa 1960s, essentially a large rectangular concrete box, sitting on a slab of asphalt. If you dropped by to visit me and you were in a polite mood, you would think it was old and tired. I work in a small office in this tired building, sitting behind an old wooden desk, with squeaky drawers that open and close with significant effort. Some weeks back, my desk became unsteady as one of the old legs started to wobble, ultimately falling off, requiring that I temporarily replace the leg with a stack of books under the failing corner. Later that day, I approached my manager, handed him the broken leg and asked if he could get me a new desk. He assured me he would take care of it the very next day. Great, I thought,*"

I'll finally get a new desk with drawers that won't stick all the time! That should help spruce up my sad looking office. The next day one of our hardware technicians knocked on my door, well that was fast I thought, he must be here to measure the space for my new desk. But, as I glanced up at him, I noticed he was holding the old wooden leg, a hammer and a bottle of Elmer's glue. 'Would you mind moving for a minute?' he asked. Then with a few quick bangs of a hammer, a little glue and two long nails, the leg of my desk was back into position, seemingly secure and stable. The technician officially announced 'good as new' on his way out of my office. And this story represents the key reason you should buy from us. Our company focuses on the things that are important to you — quality people, rapid delivery, responsive service and keen pricing. As you can see, we don't invest in first class office space, expensive furniture, plush carpeting, and other superfluous items that increase overhead without improving your pricing or service."

There was a short pause after I finished, then a chuckle from the decision maker. He said their company didn't invest in expensive furniture either, that they were a lean overhead operation. They promised to review our proposal and give us an answer the next day. And true to their word, we received a large purchase order, and this company subsequently purchased over a million of dollars from us in the ensuing year. About three years later, I bumped into one of the people from that meeting and they mentioned how much they liked that story. Though it was just another pitch from another vendor, because the pitch was made as a short, interesting and relevant story, it conveyed a clear and emotional feeling which they could embrace. Think of a way to express your benefits in terms of stories, make sure it is short and interesting and add details and metrics for optimum results.

Tip 81   Closing with Incentives

There are pros and cons to offering incentives to close a deal. Offering a qualified prospect an incentive to buy can successfully instill urgency and help close the sale. However, offering incentives can also decrease profitability and may do so unnecessarily. Carefully measure the interest of your prospect throughout your sales process. If they need a gentle nudge, perhaps you can offer a modest increase in services, faster delivery or some extra resources. Avoid price incentives whenever possible, and try to stay away from selling on price. Offer service oriented items that your prospects might value, yet don't cut into your margins in any meaningful way. This can be a win-win, showing your prospects that you want their business, but also demonstrating you have provided them a fair price and compelling value.

Tip 82   Closing with the Exploding Deal

The deal is here today, but gone tomorrow, the special terms explode or vanish after a specific deadline. Leveraging an exploding deal, a special value which will end if not purchased "soon," is a highly effective closing tool for both traditional and virtual businesses. This can be accomplished in many different ways, depending on the product, service or solution you are selling. Here are a few examples of how you could frame an exploding deal for your prospect.

- Widget inventory will be depleted by the end of the month.

- Lock in special terms which will change at the beginning of the month, quarter or year.

- My most senior project manager (installation specialist, consultant, trainer, etc.) is available for your project now, but will begin working with another client by Monday (or next week, month, etc.).

- Our pricing structure is changing and your quotation will only be valid until the 31st of this month.

- If you sign this week, I can offer you an additional complementary service.

- If you make the sales process more efficient, I'll ensure it is a win-win (offer an extra service or better terms with this leading statement).

The common theme is a deadline to execute under these special circumstances. Notice that at no point do we suggest a price decrease (only a possible minor addition of complimentary services), as we never want to disrupt the integrity of our value or margins. For certain types of sales, we do realize price incentives go with the territory, but as noted in prior Tips, we'd suggest you explore other alternatives before reverting to selling on price.

 **Power Tip**

An exploding deal is a highly effective technique, as outlined in Tip 82, but it must be used with discretion, and you must ensure it is being used at the very end of the closing process. Some argue that you have not truly succeeded in conveying your value proposition if you're resorting to incentive closing. But there are many types of buyers out there, and incentive closing has been a staple for many years across many industries. An exploding deal can be an effective closing technique, however, it is a method that also comes with certain downside risk.

For example, let's say you have successfully identified, qualified and presented to an in-profile prospect who would be an excellent client. You determine that an exploding deal would be an effective closing technique, as the decision maker has been slowly inching forward in the process. You offer to add a "something extra" to the project by slightly enhancing services, which will have a negligible impact on your costs, but will enhance the value of your offering — if they sign by end of month. But the month ends and the client failed to execute your agreement. Then, one week after the month ends, they are ready to sign and explain they were very busy and now are free to focus on your solution, and they are very excited about the inclusion of additional services. What should you do?

You can include the additional resources and sacrifice a modicum of credibility, or you can take a hard line and explain that they missed your deadline and you will no longer be able to offer these extras. The former will keep your client happy, but will train them to assume they can glean these extras at any time. The latter will establish you as credible and steadfast, but could sour the relationship. You can also offer an alternative, perhaps a different type of service might be included as a replacement incentive. Use incentives and the exploding deal when you have a prospect that needs a nudge to make a decision — but, be cautious and keenly aware of the associated risks. Once offered, it can be challenging to renege on an incentive, another good reason to use modest incentives when absolutely needed.

Tip 83   Closing with the Deferred Implementation Plan

Receiving a commitment to purchase is often easier than obtaining a signed agreement. Successfully navigating the first three phases of the 4-Phase Virtual Sales Process should give you a simple and easy path to ask for the business. Responses to your trial closing questions may be a simple yes or no. However, some prospects will offer a "yes, but" with the "but" followed by some caveat. For example, you might hear "yes, but I need to wait until next quarter" or "yes, but I need to complete a current project prior to signing." This caveat offers an excellent opportunity to close the deal using something I call the deferred implementation plan. Company executives, managers at small businesses and entrepreneurs face endless demands on their time, budget cycles, and multiple projects in their queue. The deferred implementation plan acknowledges and addresses this fact. By offering to begin at a mutually agreeable future date, you can accommodate your prospect's current obligations, which may revolve around scheduling, new solution rollout, or key person on maternity leave. No matter what their obligations are, you can provide a comfortable path to close the sale. Try leveraging the deferred implementation technique by simply stating, "You can take advantage of our deferred implementation plan locking in terms and pricing. This will guarantee that you are not faced with a price increase and provide you ample time to prepare for this project while removing the budget and timing obstacles you face this quarter." If a prospect is genuinely interested and indicated they would like to begin if they could just find the time, they are very likely to agree to this offer. In many instances, the deferred implementation plan accounted for up to 15% of my sales at any given time.

Tip 84   Closing with Peer Suggestion and Peer Pressure

Close business by explaining that many families, professionals or organizations, which are the same type and profile as your prospect, are using your solution with great success. This is particularly effective when selling into a homogenous market or industry vertical. For example, perhaps your solution has helped many top organizations and executives improve customer service response times, or reduce product returns or customer complaints. Provide them with testimonials from others in their industry. They'll see that many people or companies they know are leveraging your solution successfully and they should too. Make sure you have metrics and case studies to back up your statements to help effectively convey this message. Though this Tip may seem simple, we encounter many companies lacking written or video testimonials and case studies to leverage this technique.

Tip 85   Closing Using End-Of-Year Budget

"Use it or lose it," is a well-known saying in the sales process. At the end of each year (or fiscal year), salespeople may have a unique opportunity with their prospects. Many organizations structure budgets in a manner that resets allocations at the end of each year. For example, if a business has a marketing budget of $1,000,000, and has $150,000 left in late November, they may be motivated to spend the balance because the remaining funds are not rolled over to the next year. For many companies, if there is an end of the year departmental surplus, the balance vanishes and is transferred back to the general company coffers. Tapping into this available budget is a great way to finalize a sale or execute a pilot-to-purchase agreement (see Tip 87), which might otherwise go unfunded. When attempting to close a sale toward the end of a fiscal year, ask questions to uncover end-of-year (EOY) budget information during the last quarter. Most businesses use the calendar year as a fiscal year for simplicity, but validate this by asking when their fiscal year ends. This can be a vital piece of information allowing you to tap into "use it or lose it" funds to help land a new sale. Left over funds available near the end of year instill urgency in most sales cycles, allowing you to execute an agreement at record speed. Make sure you contact all prospects who expressed interest in your solution during the year, but failed to progress in your P2P. End of the year budgets can change both their purchase priorities and budget perspective. And remember, some companies will require delivery and payment for your solution within the given fiscal year. Make sure you allow sufficient time to consummate the sale according to the specific policy nuances of your prospect.

Tip 86 Closing Using the Pilot-to-Purchase Method

The pilot to purchase technique is referred to by some salespeople as a try and buy. However, it is highly preferable to close using a paid pilot, with a clear and simple path to purchase upon completion of the pilot. It's much easier for someone to try four months of services than commit to 12 months, or to purchase a $20,000 pilot as opposed to a $120,000 solution. Not all products, services or solutions can be offered as a pilot, but if they can, it offers an excellent path to purchase for many types of organizations, businesses and individuals.

 **Real-World Scenario**

We were recently working with a prospect who was in-profile and qualified, they were the right type of business, they were the right size, they had budget and urgency, and we were speaking with the decision maker (BUD). They seemed very interested in our marketing services, particularly our e-marketing and Web seminar lead generation program. After our second presentation, we utilized the trial close technique, and found there was great reticence from the business owner, who we'll refer to as Bob. Bob tried a marketing services engagement with another firm, but it didn't work out, and he wasted a lot of time and money. He refused to make any decision that would risk repeating this process, and made this point crystal clear during our trial close. This created a great opportunity to leverage the pilot-to-purchase closing method. We restructured our agreement from a one-year contract to a 90-day pilot with an option to continue for the remaining nine months with a simple email confirmation. Bob found this path to be much less risky and quickly agreed to begin. Our flexibility and responsiveness to his concerns helped him view us as a partner, someone who was flexible and interested in addressing their needs. Bob signed an order confirmation, and 90 days later extended his agreement for the full term. Bob became a long-term client and a quality reference for our organization.

Tip 87   Closing by Leveraging the Queue

"I understand that you would like to begin this project next month. We have an active client queue and I'd like to ensure you are provided with your preferred installation date. If you can sign this agreement by _____, we'll guarantee your preferred installation date." Leveraging a queue or delivery timetable helps instill urgency, and if done tactfully, will never appear pushy or aggressive.

Tip 88   Closing Using the Kickoff Meeting of Similar Service

When a prospect is very close to purchasing but seems reticent to sign an agreement, even a pilot-to-purchase agreement, offer them a complimentary service like a kickoff meeting. Examples of this might include a one hour management consulting review, an insurance risk assessment analysis, a basic landscape design review, a 401K portfolio diversification assessment, a free 20 minute piano lesson or even a 15 minute introductory massage. Sometimes a subtle push toward an initial action provides the necessary impetus to finalize an order. Of course you have to balance the time investment with your close ratio. If you are closing a satisfactory number of these types of opportunities, and are doing so profitably, you have another valuable closing technique for your closing phase.

Tip 89 Different Buyers Buy Differently

This sounds obvious but often becomes elusive in practice. One prospect will promise you a decision by the end of the week, and provide you with an answer on Friday morning. The next prospect will say the same thing, disappear for several weeks, only to return with a signed order confirmation. And, some prospects are never to be seen or heard from again. The vast differences in communication style and responsiveness are challenging, and need to be properly managed for you to become a competitive and effective virtual sales organization. The preeminent approach for cultivating buyers of disparate styles is to ask as many questions as possible during your web presentation and proposal delivery. How do they prefer to be contacted? When would they like you to follow up? Should you schedule a conference call or Web meeting to answer questions next week? Inquiries like this give the buyer an opportunity to tell you how they prefer to buy, giving you the knowledge needed to properly assist them in their process and minimizing the possibility of confusion and frustration. Get all of the prospect's contact information including land line, cell phone, Skype contact, link via LinkedIn, business email (and even personal email if you are involved in a long sales cycle). This information ensures you can follow-up with this contact, until you get a yes or no response. Follow up is an art and a science, try to determine how your prospect prefers to be contacted and try to respect their boundaries. Be consistent, persistent, patient and congenial. It's a balancing act, but one that is important for you to master to optimize your virtual sales efforts.

Tip 90 Revalidate Budget: Is There a CFO or Financial Hurdle?

Internal sponsors and champions have likely been told budget is available for a purchase or project, but this must be clarified and validated. In some organizations there may be an ancillary individual, such as a CFO or finance director who polices all expenditures. Ask your internal sponsor if there will be a financial review or a financial sign off that is required, even if you've had this discussion earlier in the process. If you have commitment to close, do not underestimate this step and make sure you understand where the budget is coming from and how and when it will be approved.

Tip 91   Be Prepared to be Asked for a Last Minute Discount

As noted in the prior tip, in many businesses there are often "financial police" who are responsible for monitoring all major expenditures. In some cases, this is a formal policy with an owner, a purchasing department or CFO review, while in other cases it is informal, with a senior vice president or owner who reviews any significant purchase. The financial police may appear at the time the proposal is presented, but if they do not, it does not indicate the hurdle has been cleared. Sometimes the indication comes directly from your prospect, "I've been asked to get a 10 percent discount, our CFO informed us that due to the current economic climate all vendors must offer this to be considered." Some prospects even wait until they are about to sign on the dotted line, stating they'll sign if you can shave some percentage off your proposal, or some other type of concession. Be prepared to firmly hold your ground when this occurs. Pricing integrity late in the process is no less important than it was early in the process.

Tip 92   Three Methods of Discount Deflection

There are many effective methods for dealing with a discount request. Offered in a sample conversation format, here are three methods we use and have found to be very effective.

1. **The Trade** – "I'm glad you're willing to purchase if we can provide a 10 percent price reduction. We can certainly offer that by reducing a few services and still have a highly effective project/solution."

Don't reduce price without reducing deliverables. An example of this technique is given in the first Power Tip in this chapter.

2. **The Virtual Value Story (or your value story if you're not yet virtual)** – "As a virtual organization, we have minimal overhead and expenses. Therefore, our pricing reflects only the talent and expertise we will leverage for your project. You don't pay for any overhead, and as a result you already have been given keen pricing." This is a soft approach to making a firm deflection, and reminds the prospect of your enhanced value. If you're not virtual, be prepared to demonstrate how you deliver a great value and competitive pricing.

3. **The Reverse** – As the name implies, you turn the request around as a challenge to your prospect. "If I were to offer you this discount, it would be an admission that my solution is overpriced. We already offer greater value than our competitors, which you even noted in our prior meetings. Perhaps we don't have a good fit here - or we haven't done the job needed to prove that we offer a great value." This will often force a retreat, with the prospective client admitting they were just testing price sincerity, but it does run the risk of being considered as an aggressive ultimatum.

Tip 93 Revalidate Signature Process

Ensure nothing is contrary to your sponsor's perspective of the final steps in the sales process. Confirm their expectations about the signature process or purchase order execution are accurate. Can they sign your order confirmation themselves? Do they require a legal review, multiple signatures, their managers' initials? Deep into the sales cycle, this should not be difficult to ascertain (or revalidate) and can be achieved by candidly asking your sponsor if he has discussed the signature process or met with their manager (hopefully an owner, CEO, CFO, etc.). If they have not, suggest they contact the decision maker immediately. This is in their best interest, as they do not want to risk any obstacles in procuring your offering after investing the time and effort to reach this point so close to closure.

Tip 94   Create the Final Sales Order Confirmation

Simplify the contract process and make it easy for them to sign. Make your proposals clear and concise. Include the least amount of material required to be effective. Your presentation likely included many samples and stories about how effective your solution or service will be, but cluttering your proposal with this information is repetitive and can bog down the process. Make every effort to minimize legalese (though you should run your basic legal language by a business attorney when starting your virtual business). I created an order confirmation almost 30 years ago and have used something similar ever since. Simplify your process and take a Spartan approach to your agreements whenever possible.

 **In-Depth Review**

At StartUpSelling, Inc., we created a very effective proposal methodology ensuring a fast and simple proposal and agreement process. Our standard proposal (we often refer to this as an Order Confirmation) consists of four pages:

1. Cover page

2. Service offering summary

3. Notes and terms

4. Signature page (can be combined with notes and terms as seen below)

 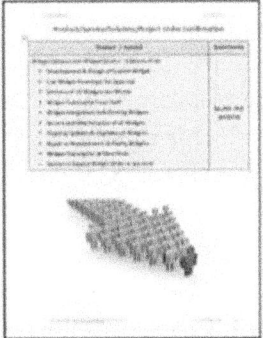 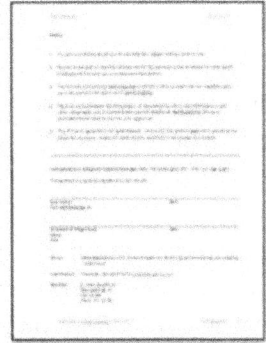

The service offering is a clear and concise list of deliverables. If more than one page of services is required, or there is greater complexity pertaining to the scope of work, we simply increase the number of service/deliverable pages to reflect what we need. This presupposes we are not proposing a larger scale six or seven figure project. Our notes and terms are typically a handful of bullets better elucidating exactly what we will deliver. We have a very simple legal, confidentiality and binding arbitration clause, and since we are a services firm we have limited IP concerns. Granted, the legal clause can vary with different types of business, but do what you can to shorten and simplify. By making each part of our proposal simple and easy to understand, we make it much easier for our prospects to sign.

Tip 95   Determine How You Will And Should Get Paid

Cash is king, and that starts with the contract process. Who gets the bill? How is it approved? Who pays and when will they pay? These items are critical to the health of your business and should be answered by the decision maker, or your internal sponsor. Once the agreement is signed, mention that you have a few brief administrative items you would like to finalize, so that your future focus can be on delivery and service, as opposed to billing and collection. Ask where to send the bill and if they require a purchase order number. For B2C sales, will they pay by credit card, check or PayPal?

Hopefully your order confirmation required a deposit, or monthly billing in advance, instead of arrears. Apartments, condo fees, insurance, cell phone bills and many other payments today are done in advance, not arrears. Depending upon your type of business, you should try to negotiate your receivables in the same way. If this type of upfront payment is not possible, ask for Net 10 terms, don't settle for Net 30 terms. Many businesses, even very large organizations will accommodate these requests. It might surprise you, but for years, many of my clients have paid 33 percent to 50 percent of their project fees up front. Some pay monthly or quarterly in advance. We pay our contractors very promptly which elicits great loyalty, and also pay for our cloud computing solutions in advance to ensure keen pricing. It's a win-win, as our clients look at us as a partner, and invest in our success, while we prioritize their needs and provide rapid response to their specific initiatives. Your business should review your billing and payment policies to optimize cash flow, and to help you deliver exceptional service.

Tip 96 Set a Time Limit for Contract Execution

Congratulations, your internal sponsor or the decision maker has given you a commitment, they are moving forward and will sign your agreement. When you receive a commitment to purchase, get a firm date for contract execution. If there is no deadline, other pressing issues will continually absorb the bandwidth of your buyer, and your contract will become an elusive prize. The best way to avoid this scenario is to instill urgency by creating a timeline for the deliverable. For example, if you have the contract by the end of the day Friday, you will queue your resources to begin Monday morning. Or, if you receive the order confirmation by 4 p.m. on Thursday, you will ship your solution overnight to arrive on Friday. The specific date and time will create a deadline for your prospect and, when properly positioned, ensuring your agreement will be a high priority as opposed to just another important item on their agenda.

Tip 97 Email Order Confirmation - Ask for a Scanned PDF

Ask for a signed, scanned attachment of the sales order confirmation via email. If your business requires a paper copy, you can also have them overnight the original. The preferred method for a virtual sales organization (and hopefully a paperless operation like StartUpSelling), is to email a PDF version of the Order Confirmation, have your prospective client sign, scan, attach and email it back. PDF's are quickly and easily created in newer versions of Microsoft Word, or with free tools like CutePDF. Some prospects may be willing to use actual digital signatures, though as of this writing, that might be a little bit leading edge for many companies. We've used the email and PDF method for many years now, and it seems to be commonly accepted by our clients, and provides a simple, fast and hassle free way to quickly finalize the agreement. Always remember to ask if they need a copy of an invoice to help expedite payment processing, while engaged in the contract execution process.

Tip 98 Contract Receipt: Get the Contract in Your Hands ASAP

Whether your receive a scanned and executed PDF, a FedEx copy or even if you have to pick it up in person (least desirable for efficient web selling) make sure you get the contract in your hand as soon as possible. Get a deposit, or a commitment that the payment is in process at that time or as soon as possible. You never know when a new corporate directive, a bad quarter, a new vice present or CEO, or imminent takeover can kill your deal.

 **Real-World Scenario**

Several years ago, I was working on a sales opportunity in England. After a long RFP process, we won the business, the sale was completed and we had a contract in hand. Much of the work was done virtually, but the final step, a formal kickoff meeting, was completed in London at the request of our new client. The kickoff meeting went well, and we assured this client, a division of a well known company, that their project would be a top priority. We received 50 percent of the project engagement fee up front, shortly after our return from London. This was to add the client to our queue, assemble a project team, review their materials and begin work on their campaigns. Then the phone call came, about three weeks after our return. It went something like this, "We've had a major shift at our company and we're closing down this division, we want to cancel the contract and get a refund." After months of work on their RFP, an on-site kickoff meeting in London, the receipt of a signed contract and their deposit, the assignment of a project team, and work in process, this client wanted to cancel and get a refund. But this would be unfair to our company, work was underway and the project team would need to be reassigned. Fortunately the request was contrary to our contract and payment terms, an important lesson in protecting your business from unforeseen circumstances. Though we released the client from further obligation, we kept the initial payment for the work which was provided and still maintained a profitable project to that point in time. As we'll see in Tip 100, deposits are helpful in many ways.

Tip 99   Get a Purchase Order Number If You Sell to Larger Businesses

If you're selling to larger companies, it's imperative that you understand their payment methods. It's often challenging to get paid from a larger company without a purchase order (PO) number, and your internal sponsor may not realize that one is required. Many salespeople consider contract execution to be the final step in the sales process, but this assumes your prospect will effectively overcome the challenge of paying a new vendor. Asking for a PO number as soon as the contract is signed will help expedite the payment process.

Tip 100   The Power of a Deposit

Don't underestimate the power of a deposit or monthly payments in advance as opposed to arrears. If you can collect a deposit or upfront payment, the possibility of a cancelled order is dramatically reduced. Once a client makes a payment, particularly if it is a larger sum or percentage of the purchase price, you become their partner instead of a vendor. For example, if you paid a deposit to a house painting company and they've been progressing slowly, you're more likely to work with them on the issue as opposed to fire them. If a business purchased a six month project and paid the first month upfront, they are very unlikely to cancel, especially if you've been responsive and professional. The real intent of deposits and upfront fees is to prevent buyer's remorse and turn your prospect into a partner. However, as mentioned in the prior Real World Scenario, deposits or upfront payments also help insulate your company from political and economic shifts which happen outside your sphere of influence. Don't underestimate the power of the deposit or the value of billing in advance instead of arrears.

 **Watch-Out Tip**

Be wary of slow payers or deferred payment terms. This can kill your company in two ways. First, it is damaging to your cash flow, increasing the likelihood that you might need to finance your receivables. The second issue is a bigger potential threat. If the client is holding a large amount of funds that are due, you have reverted back to the customer/vendor scenario as opposed to a partnership. When your client is holding your initial payment, or a large payment is in arrears, they are less likely (or less motivated) to work out a resolution if there's a problem. This may not be malicious in intent, merely an accounts payable department which is extremely slow to pay or even directed to handle receivables in a lethargic 60 day cycle. Always approach receivable issues politely with great respect, but firmly ask your internal sponsor for help. Don't assume they know about the payable issues, nor that they can resolve them. But when it comes to payables, watch them closely and guard payment term time frames judiciously. At StartUpSelling, Inc., we have a four week rule, that projects are placed on hold if a receivable is overdue beyond that timeframe. If you require deposits or payments in advance as opposed to arrears, it will often help identify a minor issue before it becomes a major problem.

Tip 101   Bonus Tip: Take Advantage of the Virtual Lifestyle!

Show me the money! But it's not all about the money; it's about the money and the time to use it. The virtual sales model allows for a more flexible and empowering lifestyle. Eliminate the commute, start and end your days when you wish, work at your optimum and most productive times and enjoy activities when and where you like. This is not to say you won't be working hard, just that you will likely enjoy a dramatic increase in scheduling and flexibility. For those of you currently commuting, you may earn a free hour or two each day, simply removing that unproductive hassle from your life. One of my contractors reduced his driving from 30,000 miles a year to 3,000 miles a year when he adopted our web based selling model and went virtual. He completely embraced Tip #1, "Put Your Car Keys on Your Desk and Leave Them There." But the virtual lifestyle needs your cooperation to work, end your days at a specific time or quit early on Fridays. Make sure you benefit from the elimination of a commute and the optimization of your peak production hours. Then enjoy the balance — go virtual, get profitable — and enjoy the lifestyle advantages!

Congratulations, you've now reviewed 101 Web Selling Tips to help you on your way toward a better, more efficient and more profitable sales operation. Do these tips seem to add up to an onerous process? Do you think you can bypass many of these steps? Not all occur in every sales cycle, even though many if not most probably should. Move on to the next chapter and begin to create your own 4-Phase Virtual Sales Process.

CHAPTER 5

Create Your Own Step-By-Step 4-Phase Sales Process

Now it's time to create your own 4-Phase Virtual Sales Process. Fill in the blanks and create a step-by-step guide to outline your unique process. Create your own Virtual Buyer Persona, and a Virtual Prospect Scorecard, to create a successful process for you and your team.

Virtual Buyer Persona

The Virtual Buyer Persona is a fun and useful tool to examine the alignment of your product or service offering and your prospective clientele. There are two ways to utilize this tool. You can conjure a buyer persona from existing clientele. For example, look at who buys your product and consider the traits they have in common. Think of your buyer persona as if you were creating a list of attributes for your ideal companion. How long a list would that be? How specific might you be about the criteria? Change the format from a list into a paragraph or two, and you have a description of your ideal companion. Now, do something very similar for your ideal customer, and you will have your Virtual Buyer Persona.

If you sell B2C, questions to develop this persona may include:

- How old is the average customer?

- If relevant, what is their gender?

- What is their education level?

- Where do they live, what city, state, region or country?

- What is their income level, or household income level?

- What is their political and social perspective?

- What is their marital status?

Your B2C Buyer Persona might read like this: "Michael is a 35-year-old financial planner, married with two young children living in an upscale suburban town, near Boston. He owns a house and has a mortgage, is most likely a democrat or independent, and drives a late model car. He travels locally because it is easier with two children and because he is investing in home improvements, though he is now thinking of a vacation in Disneyworld. His wife Mary drives an SUV, works part time while her children are in school, and is also interested in home improvements. Michael and Mary want to buy my cabinet re-facing service because: 1. It will update their kitchen quickly improving their home esthetics. 2. Because the cabinets don't have to be ripped out and replaced, it won't interfere with their routine or adversely impact their children. 3. It will improve the value of their home without a large capital outlay."

If your product is B2B, questions will be similar to those above and may include:

- What type of company do they work for?

- Is there something unique about this type of company?

- What is their title?

- What is their gender, or is this irrelevant?

- What is their location?

- What is their growth (or contraction) rate?

- What size is his/her organization (by revenue and/or employees)?

- What are the specific issues they face?

Your B2B Buyer Persona might look like this: "John Smith is 45 years old and owns an insurance agency with $5 million in revenues. He is the CEO and has 30 people working at the agency. Seventy percent of their revenues are property and casualty (P&C) related, while benefits and personal lines comprise the balance. They are located in the U.S., close to a large city and are trying to grow at least 10 percent per year. They only have a one-person marketing department and this individual is a manager, not a vice president. They are trying to improve their pipe-line and are open to outsourcing some or most of their lead generation services. They prefer working with companies they know or companies with demonstrated expertise in their industry, and they are struggling to differentiate their agency in a somewhat commoditized market. John, the CEO, is not the sole decision maker, but can likely convince other principals to invest in a marketing initiative if he so desires. John wants to buy my website development services because: 1. We work exclusively with insurance agencies. 2. We understand the keywords appropriate for an agency like yours. 3. We have many agency references and agency web-sites to ensure you are confident that we can get the job done, on time, and within budget."

Asking these questions will help you identify a more literal and tan-gible basis of your target buyer, who they are and what they want. Once you've ascertained your Virtual Buyer Persona, you will more readily cus-tomize your solution offering to the needs of your prospects and better adapt when those needs change. It often helps to actually give this buyer a name. In the examples above, they might be Michael, the financial planner, or John, the insurance CEO.

Prospect Scorecard

Your Prospect Scorecard is a standardized evaluation technique to vet prospects into qualified prospects. There are two sections in the VPS. The ideal attributes are first. These are used to determine if a prospect is in-profile and they are also known as the qualifying attributes. The second section is the Virtual Prospect Qualifier (sometimes we refer to this as just the Prospect Qualifier). Creating your own Prospect Qualifier will prove somewhat akin to developing your own Buyer Persona (as discussed above). You need to assess the relevant aspects of your prospect relationship. The Prospect Scorecard will help you focus on both prospect viability and finding the P2P (path to purchase). Like a buyer persona, this can vary quite a bit from business to business. For your Prospect Qualifier, you may use something as simple as BUD (budget, urgency, decision maker), BUN (budget, urgency, need) or BUNT (budget, urgency, need, timing). These are applicable to many businesses, whether B2B or B2C. In a business, this would address how much is available to spend, how soon the prospect wants your product, and whether or not you can effectively convey your value proposition to the person responsible for spending. In a household, this is very similar. Sometimes these qualifiers will actually be interdependent. If your solution costs above a certain threshold, the decision maker may change. Thus, a Prospect Qualifier should be performed at the inception of every potential sale, but may require modification as you learn more in the sales process. Some companies that sell more complex solutions may need to expand their acronym to accommodate a more intricate sales process, e.g., RENT (RFP, event, need, timing) or BUTANE (budget, urgency, timing, authority, need, event).

A Prospect Qualifier must be accurate without being overly cumbersome. Ensure you include the key criteria you need to close a sale, and no more. For example, if you cannot close a sale without identifying a significant budget, it should be included in your Virtual Prospect ID. For some businesses, providing a compelling hard ROI (Return on Investment) is necessary to prove your solution can pay for itself. Investigating past successes and failures in your sales history can help to shape these qualifiers. Generally, similarities between successful and failed conversions will not merit a slot in your Prospect Qualifier, while consistent differences between the successes and failures will likely be at the heart of your virtual prospect acronym. Like all things in business, adaptability here is key. You can and should refine your Virtual Prospect Qualifier after you've used it five or 10 times. If you find it had a high rate of accuracy, then it will likely work well in the future, though you should monitor the results every month or quarter. This is easy to do, compare your VPS scores against your wins and losses. If you encounter many unexpected results in your prospect meetings, one of the causes may simply be that you have overemphasized or underemphasized the importance of a qualifying factor. As you hone in on which attributes result in appointments and sales, you will be able to apply this strategy throughout the sales process.

Creating and utilizing the Prospect Qualifier should prove fast and highly valuable in helping you in the identification and qualification phases of your virtual sales process. Your Prospect Qualifier, like many aspects of your adaptable virtual business, may change over time, as you close new business and as your product and services offerings grow and change.

Go to: http://www.ProspectScorecard.com for a sample Prospect Scorecard. Additional Prospect Scorecard information is in Appendix 2.

PROSPECT SCORECARD - FOR B2B ORGANIZATIONS										Copyright StartUpSelling, Inc.
Prospect Attributes	ABC Co.	XYZ Co.	ones Corp	Smith Co.	Silver Co.	Sterling	USA Co.	Salt Inc.	Pepper Co.	Zinc Co.
$5 to $50 Million in Revenues	1	1	1	1	1			1	1	
50+ Employees	1	1		1	1			1	1	1
Located in NY or NJ	1	1	1	1	1	1	1		1	1
Target Industry Vertical(s)	1	1		1	1	1		1		1
Need for Solution Like Yours	1	1	1					1		
Open to Change/New Vendors	1	1	1	1			1	1		1
Strong Champion/Internal Sponsor	1	1	1					1	1	
Centralized Decision Making Model	1	1	1	1				1	1	1
Previous Sale or Engagement	1	1	1	1			1	1		
Referral or Cross-Sale		1	1					1		
Score *	9	10	8	7	4	2	3	7	7	5
Result	Win	Win	Win	Win	Loss	Loss	Loss	Pending	Pending	Pending
* 8-10: Ideal prospect profile and a likely win | 5-7: Good prospect but be aware of out of profile attributes | 4 or under: Need a compelling reason to go after the business										
Prospect Qualifier = BUD (Capital Letter Indicates that the qualifier has been validated)										
Budget	B	B	B	B	B	b	b	b	B	B
Urgency	U	U	U	U	u	u	u	u	U	u
Decision Maker	D	D	D	D	d	d	D	d	d	d

Worksheet: Your 4-Phase Virtual Sales Process

Now it's time to create your own 4-Phase Virtual Sales Process. Fill in the blanks to create a unique sales process for your business. Remember to review, monitor and adjust your process each month or quarter to ensure you're optimizing your time and opportunities.

I. Phase One: Identify

1) Who is the most likely buyer for your solution? Will you sell to businesses or consumers? What size business (revenue or number of employees), industries and titles will you target? What type of individual or household? Where are they located?

   _____

   _____

   _____

2) Determine your specific niche, create a bull's-eye. B2B Example: Vertical or horizontal segments such as manufacturers between 50 and 500 employees. B2C Example: Households in Virginia over $100,000 in household income.

   _____

   _____

   _____

3) What is your buyer persona? Create a short written biography of your ideal prospect. Example: John Smith is 25 years old, married, two children, owns his own home and needs my solution because...

   _____

   _____

   _____

4) Where can you find a target suspect list that includes detailed contact information and emails? Where will you store your initial data – a spreadsheet, cloud-based contact manager, or SFA?

   _____

   _____

   _____

5) What is your elevator pitch? In three sentences, explain your value proposition and key differentiators. If you are unable to explain this clearly and succinctly, stop here and practice this before moving on.

_____

_____

_____

II. Phase Two: Qualify

1) What is the budget required for your product/service/solution? How will you quickly determine if your prospect has the funds available? What questions will you ask?

_____

_____

2) Is your solution a replacement for an existing solution? If so, how will you determine if your prospect is willing and able to make a change? What are the challenges they may face in making this change and how can you assist them with this process?

_____

_____

3) What is your prospect's sense of urgency? What questions will you ask to determine this? What Virtual Sales strategies will align well with you solution to create urgency?

_____

_____

4) Who makes the decision? How many people decide? Who are they?

_____

_____

_____

5) Are there other industry-specific qualifiers? Remember to think about vertical industries that could benefit from your product or solution whenever possible.

_____

_____

_____

III. Phase Three: Present

1) What is your value proposition and what are your three key differentiators? Do you present this information clearly? How will you feature this in your presentation?

_____

_____

2) How will you clearly explain your solution without using excessive technical language (unless you're selling to a technical buyer like an engineer)? Are there stories or analogies you can leverage to simplify your explanations?

_____

_____

3) What questions will you typically receive from prospects? How can you incorporate answers into your presentation?

_____

_____

4) What are the anticipated objections and how will you overcome them?

_____

_____

_____

5) What is your call to action? How will you integrate this into the presentation?

_____

_____

_____

IV. Phase Four: Close

1) Are you prepared to ask for the business? Specifically how will you ask? Create and rehearse your trial closing and closing questions.

_____

_____

2) What final objections do you anticipate and how will you overcome them? What Virtual Closing strategies will you use to deflect pricing and contractual consideration requests?

_____

_____

3) Do you have an internal champion or sponsor? How will you help them move the process forward?

_____

_____

4) Do you anticipate budget issues? Are you able to offer incentives or flexible terms without compromising margins?

_____

_____

_____

5) How will you complete the path to purchase by ensuring the contract gets signed promptly?

_____

_____

_____

Appendix 1

Definitions of Virtual Sales and Business Terms

4-Phase Virtual Sales Process: Identify, qualify, present, and close. A means of defining and tracking your entire sales process in a simple but quantifiable manner.

Alexa: A Web information company providing search engine functionality, website traffic data, and a broad ranking system corresponding to data from these features. A useful and free tool.

Article Directories: Websites allowing users (usually via membership) to post content. Upon approval, the content is published with author biographical data and promptly crawled by search engines. Helpful for relevant backlinks and SEO.

Appointment Setting: A pipeline-building technique, often leveraging telemarketing, to set up targeted prospect appointments on specific dates and times for presentations or meetings.

Backlinks: Live or active links from other Web domains back to your own. These lend credibility to your site, though the quality of the backlinks (their own domain credibility and the anchor text of the link) is often more important than the quantity.

Bayesian Filtering and Poisoning: A statistical strategy of parsing user-selected spam by determining the probability that the user will consider the incoming message to be spam. Bayesian poisoning is a spam strategy creating messages using "trusted" or low-spam keywords mixed in with the spam message. If the email client does not determine the message to be spam, it will get past their spam filters.

Buyer Persona: The attributes of an ideal prospect are written in the form of a biography. Buyer personas can be conjured from statistics about those who show interest in a product or service, or by a company wishing to reach a certain audience. For example, if your company sold solar panels, your buyer persona might begin like this: John Smith is 35 years old, an engineer with an MBA. He has a wife and two children and would be interested in solar panels for his home because of his pro- environment views.

Canvassing: Physically disseminating your company information to your suspects or prospects in the hope of generating leads. For example, driving down Main Street and stopping at every medical office to drop off a brochure about your products. Or dropping off a brochure to homes for which you would like to provide cleaning services. This is a tedious and expensive process, and not recommended for most virtual companies.

Capital Budget: A budgeting plan for large and long-term investments, often for equipment, over a period greater than that used under an operating budget. Factors such as internal rate of return, net present value, and payback period are often used when creating capital budgets. If your company sold an expensive business software solution or equipment for a factory, it might need to be purchased with funds from a capital budget.

Close Ratio: The lead-to-customer conversion ratio. Companies should track close ratio by sales person and product and, if possible, for each major product. Close ratios can be calculated in many ways including: leads to sales (customers), demos to sales, and proposals to sales, etc.

Cloud Computing: Activities taking place on remote servers or systems using the Internet. Whether using Skype, a sales force automation solution like Salesforce.com, an online backup solution, collaborating with Google Documents, or sending emails with an Internet-based e-marketing solution, you are "in the cloud." Virtual companies should take advantage of cloud computing, removing the need for internal servers and IT staff.

Contact Management Software (CMS): Software that organizes names, phone numbers, email addresses, and other important data for outbound sales, management and tracking purposes. Think of these as a simple version of more robust sales force automation (SFA) solutions.

Conversion Ratio: The ratio of group A (higher in the sales funnel) to group B (lower in the sales funnel). Conversion ratios are often tracked for visit-to-lead, lead-to-customer (or sales), and visit-to-customer, lead-to-proposal, and proposal-to-customer.

Client Relationship Management (CRM): CRM tools are used to track and manage a company's relationship with clients and prospects. This can include SFA functions, website activity, client service, etc.

Database: A set of values, usually corresponding in some nature. In business, this generally pertains to contact information (e.g., name, phone, email, etc.).

Directory Listings: Directories exist throughout the Internet as they once did in physical form, but to a much greater extent. Many directories are free, some are fee-based. Some require application, while others are completely open. There are also vertical-specific listings (e.g., medical, law, etc.) and, of course, geographical listings. Backlinks from online directories can assist in SEO efforts, though their benefits are modest with recent search engine algorithm shifts and the negative connotation of link farms and link swapping.

Domain Names: The name of a website (the text immediately preceding the ".com" or other extension). It is important to have a simple, succinct, memorable domain, though the amount of money necessary to acquire one can vary by market.

E-marketing: Marketing electronically using emails and e-marketing engines to reach a broad or targeted audience. Opt-in e-marketing methods and following spam-related regulations is a very important aspect of e-marketing.

E-publishing: Publishing of articles, books, or other written works online via article directories like Ezine and ArticlesBase, e-book stores (e.g., Amazon), or tools like WordPress.

Go-To-Market Strategy: A crucial element of starting a successful business, this strategy defines where, when, and how your products or services will be offered.

Hosting Providers: These are the companies that register your website, store its data on servers, and make it available over the Internet. Cloud hosting solutions (in which you do not need a server or technical acumen) have become very streamlined and inexpensive over the last five years.

Local Search: Localized, area-specific search results appearing on Google and other search engines. Results appear above the "global" search results with a map identifying their location. These are generally profiles created by local companies and certified by the search engine for validity.

News Release: A modern and more accurate term for a press release. Since press releases now target bloggers, websites, directory listings, microblogs and other mediums beyond traditional press outlets, and can be sent for nominal cost or free by anyone with Internet access. Press releases are now more aptly called "news releases."

Operating or Operational Budget: An operating budget, as opposed to a capital budget, is used for ongoing payments such as maintenance operations, salaries, and interest payments. This type of budget is often easier to access than a capital budget expense when selling your solution.

Page Rank: A rank from 0 (very low traffic) to 10 (very high traffic) assigned to each page on the internet. The scale is exponential. It is easier to get from a 1 to a 5 than from a 7 to an 8. The most common page ranks are Google page ranks, though other sites employ this kind of ranking system as well.

Pipeline: Your list of prospects and opportunities, typically ranked in order of likely closes. Use the Prospect Scorecard to better qualify and quantify your pipeline opportunities.

Press Release: The act of disseminating company announcements and information (generally of a time-sensitive nature) among the press, constituents, or the general public. See "News Release" for additional information.

Prospect: A potential client, one who has sufficiently acceptable qualification attributes to be moved from a suspect status to a prospect status.

Prospect List: A list of contact information about potential clients, who may reside in a spreadsheet, database, contact manager, SFA or CRM.

Sales Force Automation (SFA): Also known as sales force management. This is a tool designed to track relationships between sales professionals and their suspects and prospects. SFA solutions can reside locally or in the cloud and can be simple contact management type solutions or more sophisticated solutions incorporating email marketing and other advanced functions.

Search Bots: The automated programs that scour the web to identify and index site content. More relevant and dynamic content is theoretically more trusted content, and search bots are supposed to allow search engines like Google to render the best matches on their search engine result pages (SERPs). Search engines are far from perfect and the results can, and will, vary.

Search Engines: Websites or Web tools that employee a database and an algorithm to filter through the content of the Web, retrieving results based upon user query. Google, Bing and Yahoo! are currently some of the best known search engines.

Search Engine Marketing (SEM): A series of marketing techniques centered around success through Web visibility via SERPs. This includes on-page SEO (title, keywords, descriptions, content), off-page SEO (articles, YouTube, backlinks), social media propagation of content (Twitter, StumbleUpon, Digg), and PPC/CPC (paid results on search engines such as Google).

Search Engine Optimization (SEO): This is the process of making Web pages more attractive to search engines, and can be achieved through a combination of on-page (titles, keywords, content, etc.) and off-page (articles, backlinks, social media, etc.) efforts.

Search Engine Results Page (SERP): When users type in a search query, like "high definition plasma TVs" or "Web marketing agencies," search engines like Google, Bing and Yahoo! return results pages with related Web links ranked, theoretically, in order of relevance. On the top of the results page are often paid advertisements (PPC Ads), the organic results are in the middle of the page, under the paid ads.

Search Marketing Optimization: Another term for SEO or SEM.

Small Office/Home Office (SOHO): SOHO refers to small or home-based businesses, increasingly more common with the adoption of virtual business methodologies.

Social Media Marketing: The process of sharing information about your company, or information that will draw attention to your company, leveraging Web technologies. There are many social media tools currently in broad use, including Twitter, Facebook, YouTube, StumbleUpon, Digg, LinkedIn, WordPress and others. Using these tools is relatively simple, but creating a coordinated effort, achieving optimum recognition and positively influencing SERP requires great understanding and skill for most types of companies.

Software as a Service (SaaS): This is a form of cloud computing solution in which software is hosted and accessed remotely by the end user, usually under membership (periodic payment) instead of licensing (one-time payment). An example of this is Google Documents, a free cloud computing solution. SalesForce.com is another example, which is a fee-based solution.

Spam: Unsolicited email, usually filled with deceptive content and attempts to get the user to click through to a bogus or nefarious website for the purposes of advertising income, email address theft, etc.

Spam Filters: Sorting algorithms that attempt to identify the quality of an email employing various metrics like sender, body text, and more.

Suspect: Any business or consumer in your general target market profile.

Suspect List: List of businesses or consumers with all relevant contact information for your target market. These suspects are theoretically in-profile, but are not considered prospects until such time as they are further qualified.

Telemarketing: Calling suspects or prospects in an attempt to convert them into leads or customers. Telemarketing can incorporate telesales, appointment setting, prospect qualification or even survey research services.

Telesales: Another term for telemarketing.

Virtual: Any business or activity conducted outside of physical proximity to the collaborating parties.

Prospect Scorecard: A tool, created by StartUpSelling, Inc., for evaluating prospect profiles and their likelihood to purchase. The Prospect Scorecard quantifies prospect pipelines and replaces arbitrary terms or rankings with quantifiable and measurable metrics.

Web Marketing: The process of reaching out to suspects and prospects virtually and digitally, rather than with physical media, such as brochures, snail mail, canvassing, physical trade shows, newspaper ads or other traditional marketing means. This includes email marketing, webinar marketing, the various forms of SEM, PPC and other Web-based ads, etc.

Web Meetings: Interactive Web-based meetings that take place online, using tools like GoToMeeting to connect with prospects, clients, and colleagues at any distance. Some consider tools like Skype also to be Web-based meeting solutions.

Web Seminars (Webinars): Similar to Web meetings, but utilized in a one-to-many setting, where a speaker(s) addresses a topic to a larger audience that listens but does not engage verbally. Attendees are typically muted during a webinar, listening to the speaker and watching PowerPoint type presentations on their PCs. Microsoft, IBM, Adobe, GoToWebinar (Citrix) and Webex are major names currently associated with Web seminars.

Appendix 2

Using the Prospect Scorecard: Quality Score and Virtual Prospect Qualifier

How do you create and use the Prospect Scorecard? It's important to quantify the quality of your prospects. First, you need to find a formula that will help guide you to invest time and money with people and/or companies who are more likely to buy. Ensure your team is all speaking the same language, turning vague prospect terms like "hot," "warm" or "good" into quantifiable terms like "8," and "BUD qualified." Creating a Prospect Scorecard will help you accomplish this, allowing you to successfully measure your entire pipeline and each opportunity within your pipeline. Go to www.ProspectScorecard.com for more information on this tool and to download Excel and mobile app versions of the Prospect Scorecard.

PROSPECT SCORECARD - FOR B2B ORGANIZATIONS										Copyright StartUpSelling, Inc.
Prospect Attributes	ABC Co.	XYZ Co.	Jones Corp	Smith Co.	Silver Co.	Sterling	USA Co.	Salt Inc.	Pepper Co.	Zinc Co.
$5 to $50 Million in Revenues	1	1	1	1	1			1	1	
50+ Employees	1	1		1	1			1	1	1
Located in NY or NJ	1	1	1	1	1	1	1		1	1
Target Industry Vertical(s)	1	1		1	1	1		1		1
Need for Solution Like Yours	1	1	1						1	
Open to Change/New Vendors	1	1	1	1			1		1	1
Strong Champion/Internal Sponsor	1	1	1					1	1	
Centralized Decision Making Model	1	1	1	1				1	1	1
Previous Sale or Engagement	1	1	1	1			1	1		
Referral or Cross-Sale		1	1					1		
Score *	9	10	8	7	4	2	3	7	7	5
Result	Win	Win	Win	Win	Loss	Loss	Loss	Pending	Pending	Pending
* 8-10: Ideal prospect profile and a likely win	5-7: Good prospect but be aware of out of profile attributes	4 or under: Need a compelling reason to go after the business									
Prospect Qualifier = BUD (Capital Letter indicates that the qualifier has been validated)										
Budget	B	B	B	B	B	b	b	b	B	B
Urgency	U	U	U	U	u	u	u	u	U	u
Decision Maker	D	D	D	D	d	d	D	d	d	d

The Quality Score (noted as Score on the Scorecard) in your prospect scorecard is used to determine if you are fishing in the right pond, if your prospect is within your target profile. Let's say you create a 10-point scale for your Quality Score (the ideal client prospect would score "10" out of a possible "10" from the attributes you've selected), and you are working with a prospect who scores a "9" on that scale, therefore, you know you are working with an in-profile prospect. From a profile prospective, the prospect is clearly worthy for you to invest time and resources. They are much more likely to purchase than someone who scores a "3" out of "10." You might come up with a general rule that you want 90 percent of your prospects to be a "7" or better so they appear as top pipeline opportunities. This doesn't mean you refuse to engage with someone who scores "3" out of "10," however, you will be wary of your investment, measuring your investment against the likelihood of an ultimate close. And remember, you don't have to use a 10-point scale, you can use five, seven or any point system you like. Although we strongly suggest you not exceed a maximum of 10 so you can easily manage your scoring system.

To determine the likelihood of closing, you should create a Virtual Prospect ID, your qualifying acronym to help you determine the probability of closing your deal. Simpler is better should be your mantra, a short qualifying acronym like BUD often works well. BUD stands for budget, urgency and decision maker. In many sales processes, if you have these three elements, your much more likely to close a sale. Other acronyms might include BUNT (budget, urgency, need, timing) or BUTANE for a more complex sale (budget, urgency, timing, authority, need, event). Try RICE (ROI, IT sponsor, capital, event) or even SPIN (service, pain, initiative, need). Think about the three to six key elements in your closing process, and how they align and culminate into a signature. If you can simplify and clarify, you will provide yourself and others much better visibility into your pipeline, your sales process and the likelihood of upcoming closes.

Once you have created a Quality Score and Prospect Qualifier, you can measure your current prospects against prior deals, both wins and losses. This accomplishes two things, it validates correct Prospect Scorecard criteria and, if you have concerns about certain elements, it allows you to change them. For example, if you notice you are closing far more sales in a particular vertical (let's say banks), you might want to make that attribute part of your Quality Score. Ultimately, you need to be confident that a high Quality Score (9 out of 10) and a perfect Prospect Qualifier (BUD) is extremely likely to result in a sale. What is a reasonable closing ratio in this case? Though it depends on your business, a prospect in the center of your bull's eye when you are working with the decision makers should be double your normal close ratio. If your overall close ratio is 30 percent, you should close at least 60 percent of your ideal profile prospects.

Let's look at a sample Virtual Prospect Qualifier, in this case we'll review one we created called "BUD."

Budget is crucial whether you're selling landscape design or business software. Budget questions should be asked as early as possible in the sales process, differentiating a want from a true need.

- "Do you have any idea what a project like this might cost?"

- "Is this a budgeted initiative?"

- "Have funds been allocated for this project?"

- "Has it been determined which cost center will cover this procurement?"

- "Have you ever purchased anything like this before at this company?"

- "Why have you not purchased one of these yet?"

Naturally, you wouldn't ask all of these questions at one time, but if you can determine if there is budget, or where it would come from, early enough in the process, you can do a much better job of qualifying those prospects who are likely to buy from those who merely hope to buy.

Urgency is a great catalyst for purchases large and small. For large-scale procurements, urgency can often result in someone finding budget even though it may not exist at initial discussions about your solution. At CTS, we delivered custom training solutions for enterprise rollouts. If there was an impending rollout of an enterprise CRM system for example, there would be a rollout deadline and the resulting urgency. Even if budget is not sufficiently allocated, these companies would find the money because they had to complete training by the go-live date. If you are providing catering services and speaking with a prospect who is running behind for their wedding planning, you can tap into that urgency (remember the reverse timeline) and close the sale quickly. If you can identify urgency, your virtual sales process will move along rapidly. Find the urgency and close the deal.

Decision makers can make or break your sale. Are you working with an owner, CEO or CFO? In that case, you're in great shape. Or, are you at the director or manager level? Even a CEO might have to run a large-scale purchase by the board of directors. What's the process for your internal sponsor to get approval? Have they ever purchased something like this before? Are they truly a decision maker? Who signs the agreement? Do they have a formal legal or procurement process? Even a CFO of a $75 million company may lack the ability to make a decision to buy a $95,000 solution without consulting other C-level executives. Yet, in some organizations, a manager can move forward with large purchases. Make sure both you and your sponsor understand the process as you move forward in the sales cycle; and you should know who the real decision maker is. For smaller sales, you must determine if you are speaking with a shopper (the daughter who wants to buy a new coat) versus the buyer (the parent who is actually buying the coat). As with all small sales, you need to ascertain this quickly if conversing over the phone, or as a partially or completely automated qualification process through your website.

In the example above, if budget, urgency and decision maker have been identified, and your prospect is in-profile (e.g., let's say a 9 out of 10 on the Prospect Scorecard) you now have a quantifiably excellent sales opportunity.

Digg is a trademark of Digg Inc.
Wikipedia is a registered trademark of the Wikimedia Foundation, Inc.
Yahoo! is a registered trademark of Yahoo! Inc.
LinkedIn is a registered trademark of LinkedIn Corporation
Hoovers is trademark of Hoover's Inc.

Though there are many important concepts, methodologies and strategies included in the book, it's best to consult a competent attorney, CPA, or business advisor when it comes to the legal and financial aspects of your business.